# HIGH PRINCIPLE, LOW POLITICS, AND THE EMERGENCE OF THE SUPREME COURT

# HIGH PRINCIPLE, LOW POLITICS, AND THE EMERGENCE OF THE SUPREME COURT

Frederic Reynold

Wildy, Simmonds & Hill Publishing

ISBN: 9780854902835

British Library Cataloguing in Publication Data

A catalogue record for this book is available from the British Library

Wildy, Simmonds & Hill Publishing
Wildy & Sons Ltd
Lincoln's Inn Archway
Carey Street
London WC2A 2JD
www.wildy.com

Printed in Great Britain by Ashford Colour Press
Unit 600, Fareham Reach, Fareham Road,
Gosport, Hampshire PO13 0FW.

# CONTENTS

## ACKNOWLEDGEMENT

In writing this book, I have had the opportunity to talk to several people who have all played some part in the story. I am enormously grateful to each of them for giving freely of their time.

Frederic Reynold

# PREFACE

Some years ago Oxford University Press published a book to mark the demise of – to use the customary shorthand – the House of Lords as the final court of appeal, and to which many distinguished lawyers contributed individual chapters. It was the sort of weighty tome one "dipped into." I happened to dip into a chapter containing an account of the sequence of events leading to the establishment of the UK Supreme Court, entitled *From Appellate Committee to Supreme Court: a narrative*, written by Professor Andrew Le Sueur. It contained a great deal of factual information and scholarly footnotes. The thought struck me then that this episode in our contemporary history deserved slightly more expansive treatment: it seemed to me a classic instance of how a policy or a political decision of historical significance can be the result of a quite fortuitous combination of circumstances. Furthermore, one suspected that the circumstances and events which led to the emergence of the Supreme Court were not without their entertaining aspects; and crucially they could now be viewed in the light of how that court has "performed" in the first ten years of its existence.

Knowing personally some of the leading characters in the story, I have succumbed to the temptation to administer that "more expansive treatment" myself. This is not intended to be a work of scholarship but, I hope, a readable account of interest to the general reader. In the majority of instances, the source of a quotation or particular factual detail will be obvious. Where it is not, I am afraid it must be treated as "private information". Confidences must be respected.

Frederic Reynold
6 August 2019

# PART ONE
# A Rumbling Campaign and a Startling Outcome

## EARLY SIGNS

"There is to be a Supreme Court of the United
Kingdom." Thus spake section 23, sub-
section (1) of the Constitutional Reform Act
2005, – in terms rather reminiscent of the Old Testament:
"God said "Let there be light" and Lo, there was light."
Was it really as simple as that? Of course it was not.
It could not possibly have been so when, as was the
case, it involved the creation of an entirely new court
at the very apex of our legal system and the discarding
of a unique and rather quaint institution which was
acknowledged to have functioned extremely well and
to have commanded great respect throughout the
common law world. (Distinguished visiting judges
and lawyers from abroad greatly enjoyed the bonus
of a conducted tour around the Palace of Westminster
rather than experiencing simply a functional *Palais
de Justice*.) Nor could it have been so simple when
there had been no mention of such a bold project in
the election manifesto of the government which was
to be responsible for carrying out this constitutional
*coup*. Nonetheless it is a remarkable fact that now after
ten years of eventful decision-making, the Supreme
Court appears to have become a seamless part of our
constitutional fabric. What follows is the curious story
of how and why this came about, and a brief account of
how in fact the court has fared over the first ten years

of its existence. But one first needs to remind oneself of the fact that the way things were ordered at the highest level of our judiciary at the turn of this century was distinctly odd. That description will strike few lawyers and students of our constitution as being even remotely controversial. Two features stood out, both in the fullness of time becoming inextricably bound up together in the way events were to unfold.

In the first place, the highest court in the judicial hierarchy was not in fact a court but a committee – the Appellate Committee of the House of Lords, usually referred to by both the general public and the media as the House of Lords, and by the legal profession simply as "the Lords". (Indeed, as was pointed out more than once in the Parliamentary debates which were to take place later, one of its undoubted charms was that its proceedings resembled those of a seminar rather those of a courtroom.) The House of Lords had somehow over the centuries contrived to retain the role of the country's final court of appeal as well as being part of the legislature, and the Appellate Committee was its judicial "arm". Its members were the Lords of Appeal in Ordinary[1], commonly known as "the Law Lords", invariably lawyers and judges of the highest calibre. On appointment they were given life peerages, with all the rights and privileges this entailed. Their full complement numbered twelve, and they usually sat as a panel of five, very occasionally as seven, and in two notable instances as nine. They did not wear robes. They would hear the appeals in either Committee Room 1 or Committee Room 2, and very occasionally when Parliament was in recess, (– in

---

[1] The title was created by a late Victorian statute: the term "Ordinary" was used because their salary came out of the Consolidated Fund and not from Parliamentary funds.

order symbolically to underline the point that they were after all *a committee of the House of Lords*) – they would hear appeals in the Chamber itself. This arcane constitutional arrangement at the apex of our legal system pointed up a remarkable paradox: our highest and most prestigious court was the court which was the one which was the least accessible to the public. Frances Gibb, the long-serving legal correspondent of *The Times*, recently recalled how on many occasions she had difficulty in navigating her way to one or other of the two committee rooms when covering an appeal; nor for that matter was it entirely straightforward for members of the Bar, for whom their clerks had to obtain passes in advance of the hearing. As far as the general public was concerned, to find one's way to Committee Room 1 or 2 was a major initiative test.

Since the 1970s, the Law Lords had occupied rooms on the second floor of the west wing of the Palace of Westminster known as the Law Lords' Corridor. Prior to this their accommodation, following an increase in their number, had become so seriously cramped that in the mid-nineteen sixties a determined effort was made to move them out of the Palace of Westminster altogether. (Apparently some of their lordships suffered the indignity of inhabiting windowless rooms.) Ironically in the light of subsequent events, memos between the Parliamentary authorities were actually exchanged with a view to moving out the Law Lords and "the entire judicial apparatus" to the Middlesex Guildhall in Parliament Square, but eventually in December 1965 the then Clerk of Parliaments, Sir David Stephens, put a stop to such speculation. He said there was a danger of such a move resulting in the Appellate Committee being regarded as "an outdoor committee, an adjunct or outstation, rather than an integral part of the House [of

Lords}", and [horror of horrors!] it could indeed easily become a supreme court of appeal on its own."[2] (Some thirty years later another attempt was made to made to move the Law Lords out of the Palace of Westminster, this time to the recently vacated Public Record Office, an imposing late Victorian building in Chancery Lane. However, a significant number of the then Law Lords were less than impressed by the accommodation on offer, and the idea was quietly dropped.)

The second curious feature which stood out at the apex of our judicial system at the turn of this century was the pivotal role of that extraordinary figure – the Lord Chancellor. He famously had three roles. He was the actual head of the Judiciary, and as such was responsible for the appointment of all senior judges and by virtue of the same late Victorian statute which created Lords of Appeal, entitled, should he choose, to preside in any hearing of the Appellate Committee itself. He was also a senior member of the cabinet, responsible for the running of a Department of State with an ever – expanding budget. And he also presided as Speaker of the House of Lords. When the Labour government came to power in 1997 the Lord Chancellor was Lord Irvine of Lairg, popularly known in both legal and political circles as "Derry". Close successively to Neil Kinnock, John Smith and Tony Blair, he had enjoyed a substantial practice at the Bar in commercial, trade union and employment law; and having an abundance of intellectual energy he thought quite understandably that he was capable of wearing all three hats with perfect aplomb. He even contrived to chair more than one cabinet committee, as well as taking an active interest in other matters such

[2]   Quoted in *The Judicial House of Lords 1876-2009* (OUP) edit. Blom Cooper *et al.*.

as the reform of the legal aid system and the making of judicial appointments. (Eventually this versatility – or rather, hyperactivity, would contribute to his abrupt departure from office.)

Initially, what many regarded as the fault lines inherent in these bizarre constitutional arrangements continued to escape much critical attention. Discussion of such matters had largely been confined to a few eminent academics with an expertise in constitutional law. And what was of primary concern to the new Labour government was, as they saw it, the pressing need to reform the House of Lords as a legislative chamber, and specifically to remove the hereditary peers. In the time-honoured way it set about tackling the problem by appointing a Royal Commission. However, significant signs of discontent had begun to emerge, and in particular concerns had begun to be raised as to the implications of Article 6 of the European Convention of Human Rights now that the Convention had become incorporated into our domestic law by virtue of the Human Rights Act. (Article 6 required that in determining an individual's civil rights or any criminal charges brought against him or her, the tribunal hearing the matter must be "independent and impartial.")

The first of these significant signs came from that highly respected pressure group for law reform, *Justice*, (spearheaded by the former chairman of the Bar, Lord Alexander of Weedon QC, and that assiduous and effective human rights campaigner, Lord Lester of Herne Hill QC). It submitted a memorandum of evidence to the Royal Commission on Lords reform, in which it argued that that as a result of the growth in judicial review cases and the need to implement the Human Rights Act (and therefore Article 6), there was a need to separate judicial functions from those of the legislature and the executive. It therefore recommended that a supreme court should replace the Appellate Committee of the House of Lords "with its own premises, resources and staff"; that the Lord Chancellor should no longer be head of the judiciary and be entitled to sit as a judge; and that there should be an independent commission to advise on judicial appointments. These proposed changes, *Justice* argued, "[was] not a luxury but an urgent practical necessity."

That all this would in due course come to pass (albeit not with the degree of urgency which *Justice* had in mind) must have seemed a very remote possibility at the time. Particularly so, since although the future of the Law Lords, let alone that of the Lord Chancellor, was not really within its terms of reference, the Royal Commission had concluded that "there was no reason why the [House of Lords] should not continue to exercise its judicial function". Its report did however sound something of a cautionary note. It recommended that in the interests of clarity the "[Law Lords] should set out in writing and publish a statement of the principles which they intend to observe when participating in debates and votes in the second chamber and when considering their eligibility to sit on related cases." The recently appointed Senior Law Lord, Lord Bingham, duly obliged, stating that the Law Lords "did not think it appropriate to engage in matters where there is a strong element of political controversy; and…would bear in mind that they might render themselves ineligible to sit judicially if they were to express an opinion on a matter which might later be relevant to an appeal."

Derry Irvine was quick to pick up on the criticisms coming from the direction of *Justice* as well as on rumblings from elsewhere. Answering questions in the House of Lords, he rejected any suggestion that the judicial role of the Lord Chancellor should be significantly reduced. Not prone to understatement, he declared that "[t]he value of the office is that it both upholds judicial independence and mediates between the executive and the judiciary when occasion for controversy arises." This the Lord Chancellor could do, he explained, because of his seniority in cabinet and because he was head of the judiciary "and sits as such from time in the chair in important appeals." He was at pains to emphasise that in this country we did not apply strictly the doctrine of the separation of powers, and that "we fashion our constitutional arrangements pragmatically." And when speaking at the World-Wide Common Law Judiciary Conference in Edinburgh a few weeks later, he went out of his way to mount a spirited defence of the *status quo* in respect of the position of the Law Lords. He pointed out that they "made a distinctive contribution to the work of the House of Lords in debates on the administration of justice", and a specialist contribution to the work of some of its committees. There was no need to change a beneficial system, "since we do not apply the doctrine of Separation of Powers strictly." Nor, in his view, did Article 6 "require us to change our constitutional arrangements." What it required was simply a fair and impartial hearing. Provided a Law Lord in the course of a debate had refrained from expressing a concluded view on an issue later coming before him judicially, there would be no breach of Article 6. He would return to this theme more than once when speaking in the House of Lords, pointing out that the system worked well and, importantly, was cost effective. Unsurprisingly, this continued to be the government's position on the issue, and following publication of the Royal Commission's report in January 2000, the Government white paper on Lords reform stated that it "was committed to maintaining judicial membership of the House of Lords."

## THE CAMPAIGN GATHERS PACE

On 6 June 2000 Derry Irvine appointed Lord Bingham, formerly the Lord Chief Justice, to the newly created position of Senior Law Lord,[3] an appointment which was to have some unintended consequences. Lord Bingham commanded enormous respect in government circles as well as within the profession, very much a man of deeply held principles who invariably brought a scholarly historical perspective to bear on the subject in hand. He held firm views on a number of issues. In due course he was to come to hold a firm view on the need for a supreme court for the United Kingdom, whilst acknowledging that the government (– he obviously had Irvine in mind) and some of his fellow Law Lords disagreed.

A little more than a year after his appointment he used the platform of the annual lecture sponsored by *Justice* to express that view loudly and clearly, invoking what he described as the principle of judicial independence.[4] His main point was that "our institutional structure should reflect reality": if the appellate committee of the House of Lords was for

---

[3] Previously, this position was unofficial, and simply reflected seniority of length of service.
[4] Someone should one day write a monograph on the importance of the lecture as a tool used by eminent judges for influencing public opinion – a discernible trend ever since the former Lord Chancellor in the Thatcher and John Major governments, Lord Mackay of Clashfern, relaxed the rules which had previously prevented them from coming out of their shells.

all practical purposes a court acting as the supreme court of the United Kingdom and as such entirely independent of the legislature, "then it should be so established [so] as to make clear its purely judicial role and its independence". The present position could mislead and misinform.

He also gave a practical reason for establishing a separate supreme court, having clearly been less than impressed on his arrival as senior Law Lord by the facilities and accommodation available on the Law Lords corridor.[5] He pointed to the extremely cramped conditions under which they operated, a situation which, he said, did not reflect any spite or malevolence on the part of the Parliamentary authorities but the fact that the House of Lords "is after all a branch of the legislature" and in terms of space priority had to be given to those engaged in legislative work. "The needs of the legislators come first …. [This] is not unreasonable. What is unreasonable … is that decisions affecting the administration of justice at the highest level should be made by those who have no responsibility and no primary concern for the proper functioning of our [highest] court." He reflected that it was likely that in the end pressure of space could be decisive and that constitutional reform could prove "to the child of administrative necessity." An entry at this time in the published diaries of the former Law Lord (and later Deputy President of the Supreme Court) Lord Hope, both underlines the point about pressure of space within the Palace of Westminster, and the

[5]   The full complement of 12 Law Lords were accommodated in 11 rooms, a state of affairs which was only manageable because one of their number, Lord Saville, was presiding over the Bloody Sunday enquiry in Londonderry. There was no library or conference room, and only a maximum of four judicial assistants could be accommodated.

existence of divided views among the Law Lords about a supreme court:

> "The House authorities are keen to get us to move out into new premises – just as much as Tom Bingham is to see us removed from the House of Lords altogether and to set up a UK supreme court. I am not in favour of either, for purely selfish reasons. I do not believe that we can have a better working environment than we have now, or as convenient or as enjoyable a setting in which to work…. Fortunately Derry is against the idea, on the very sensible ground of cost…"

(Perspectives of course can change in the light of a change of circumstances: an earlier diary entry at the time when Lord Hope was first appointed a Law Lord describes the room he then occupied as being "only just habitable.")

Lord Bingham's comments did not exactly fall on stony ground. Within a month or so following the lecture, a liberal Democrat MP asked the Parliamentary Secretary to the Lord Chancellor's Department on the floor of the House of Commons whether "the highest court in the land [was] not compromised by its position in the legislature", and was it not "time to establish a supreme court clearly separate from the Houses of Parliament". And shortly afterwards the government published a white paper outlining further proposals for House of Lords reform in response to the Royal Commission report, in which it pointed out that the "introduction of a separate supreme court would be a major change in its own right and would deserve separate dedicated consideration", thus explicitly recognising the establishing of a supreme court as a realistic option for future discussion. Indeed, work on "contingency plans" for such an eventuality was quietly undertaken within the Lord Chancellor's Department itself just in case the government decided to change its position on the issue.

Then a month or so later the House of Commons Public Administration Committee (chaired by the Liberal Democrat MP Alan Beith, and which included the former Labour Solicitor General, Ross Cranston), reported on a number of issues into which it had been enquiring relating to reform of the House of Lords, stating that although the Royal Commission had recommended that the Law Lords should continue to sit in the Lords, the committee had been "impressed by the very different views expressed by the senior Law Lord, Lord Bingham, who recently raised the issue of whether it was desirable that the second chamber should address judicial functions at all." It had also noted his complaint as to the Law Lords' cramped working conditions. Echoing his call for the creation of a separate supreme court, it recommended that "the Law Lords should leave the second chamber at the next general election but one, [which] should allow plenty of time to think through the consequences....and to make the necessary provision for an independent, properly constituted supreme court." Reports by select committees rarely have any lasting impact, and this report could hardly have been said to have caused any ripple of excitement at the time. What it did show, however, was that the issue of a supreme court was now very much on the radar of Westminster politicians: in due course the select committee would get to hear oral evidence from Lord Bingham himself (as well as from other serving Law Lords) on the subject.

In his *Justice* lecture Lord Bingham had also discussed the anomalous tripartite role of the Lord Chancellor. Here he was at some pains not to push for any reform, prizing the Lord Chancellor's position as both a senior cabinet minister and a respected lawyer as a guarantor "of the values of the legal system and the rule of law." (As to the Lord Chancellor's role in respect of the making of judicial appointments, he was not particularly impressed by the case for replacing one man of "discernment and experience" with a body necessarily involving an entire group of decision-makers.) He evidently did not see the issues of a supreme court and reform of the office of Lord Chancellor as being part and parcel of the same problem, but it has to be borne in mind that his personal relationship with Derry Irvine was one of great mutual respect, and presumably Lord Bingham was more than alive to the sensitivities involved. After all, it was Lord Irvine who had only fifteen months previously appointed him senior Law Lord. However, his close ally and fellow Law Lord, Lord Steyn, had no such inhibitions.

Like Lord Bingham, Johan Steyn was an outstanding lawyer and scholar, who had clear and firm views on many legal issues of the day. He was born and brought up in South Africa, practised at the Cape Town Bar, eventually being appointed a senior counsel. In the early Seventies, because of his opposition to apartheid, he chose to settle in this country, and joined the English Bar. Thereafter his promotion to the High Court Bench and successively to the Court of Appeal and the House of Lords had been rapid. He was later to achieve national prominence when in the course of delivering a public lecture he strongly criticised the holding of detainees in Guantanamo Bay. On the 1st March 2002 he delivered the inaugural Neill lecture (named after Lord Neill of Bladen QC) at All Souls College, Oxford, entitled *The case for a Supreme Court*. This, in conjunction with another lecture by Lord Bingham delivered two months later, was to have repercussions. Lord Steyn developed his argument in meticulous detail and with considerable forensic skill. He started the lecture by first highlighting the oddities of the *status quo*:–

> "In 2002 the highest court in the land is still a committee of the legislature. Since 1947 it has been called the Appellate Committee. It has the appearance of a subordinate part of the Upper House. [Its] sittings therefore take place in a Committee room in the Palace of Westminster…..
> [Its] … status is underlined at the beginning of each legal year when it sits for a week in the chamber of the House of Lords. A regular reminder of its status is also the theatrical performance in the chamber [when judgment is delivered]" [6]

This state of affairs, pointed out Lord Steyn, was "the foundation of two striking anomalies in our constitutional arrangements, *viz.* that the Lord Chancellor may participate in judicial business, and that serving Law Lords may speak on legislative business in the House of Lords." He went on to pose the question: "Is there any principled, practical or pragmatic reason to retain the link between the legislature and the highest court? Do the existing arrangements have any [real] value or would it be better to strip away the legislative façade and create a

---

[6] This would take the form of a vote adopting the motion "that the report of the appellate committee be agreed to.", each of the participating Law Lords indicating in turn the order he would make.

true Supreme Court?" He was of course to answer the first of these questions with an emphatic No, and the second with an emphatic Yes.

What caused a stir and aroused a good deal of media interest was the cornerstone of his argument: namely, that the "major obstacle to creating a Supreme Court [was] the privilege of the Lord Chancellor of sitting in the Appellate Committee of the House of Lords"; that his participation in the highest court no longer served a useful purpose and was contrary to the public interest; and that the only reason for preserving the privilege of serving Law Lords to participate in the legislative business of the second chamber was "to keep afloat the Lord Chancellor's anomalous privilege of sitting in the Appellate Committee." The notion that the Lord Chancellor's combined political and judicial roles was justified on the pragmatic ground that he was able to represent the interests of the judiciary in cabinet and to represent the views of the Cabinet to the judiciary was, Lord Steyn argued, completely specious. "The judiciary does not need 'a representative' in cabinet" he pointed out. "In no other constitutional democracy does the judiciary have 'a representative' in cabinet", and in any case the Lord Chancellor was subject to collective responsibility and in no position to act as an impartial arbiter." He noted in passing that that the Lord Chancellor had not recently come to the defence of the judges when they came under repeated attack from the then Home Secretary (David Blunkett) for alleged excessive interference with government decisions: after all, one senior cabinet minister could not be seen to cross swords with another. Nor, observed Lord Steyn, did having a member of the cabinet as the head of the judiciary and sitting occasionally in the Appellate

Committee of the House of Lords in any way serve or enhance the interests of the judiciary.

He responded to Lord Irvine's mantra "We are pragmatists, not purists", by pointing out that ultimately the stability of our democratic institutions depended "on public confidence in the way in which the three co-ordinate branches of government carry out their functions .... [T]he judiciary can effectively fulfil its role only if the public has confidence that the courts ... act wholly independently." He went on to pose the rhetorical question: "What must [the public] make of the fact that in the highest court a member of the Government participates in judicial decision-making?"

The *Daily Telegraph's* headline above a full report of the lecture was typical: "Lord Irvine attacked by Senior Judge". (Clearly this is how the Permanent Secretary in the Lord Chancellor's Department, Sir Hayden Phillips, saw it, since he chose to write to Lord Steyn a personal letter of complaint.) Then barely two months later Lord Bingham re-joined the fray, delivering a lecture to the Constitutional Unit of University College, London. This was markedly different in tone from Lord Steyn's Oxford lecture, and wholly silent on the subject of the position of the Lord Chancellor.

The lecture was straightforwardly entitled: "A New Supreme Court for the United Kingdom." Lord Bingham said he profoundly disagreed with those who argued that a case for change had not been made out. "To modern eyes", he observed, "it was always anomalous that a legislative body should exercise judicial power .... This anomaly may not have mattered in the past. But if the House of Lords is to be reformed, and even if it is not, the opportunity should be taken

16

to reflect in institutional terms what is undoubtedly true in functional terms, that the Law Lords are judges not legislators, and do not belong in a House to whose business they can make no more than a slight contribution." This view, he pointed out, was based on the simple premise that the world has changed and institutions should change with it. However, Lord Bingham's central point on this occasion was that the case law recently developed by the European Court of Human rights showed that a stricter view was now being taken not only of anything which in fact may undermine the impartiality of a judicial tribunal but also of anything which might, on its face, *appear* to do so. In other words, Article 6 of the Convention was "concerned with risks and appearances as well as actualities."

He was at pains to point out that his notion of a supreme court for the United Kingdom did not involve such court exercising the sweeping constitutional powers such as those exercised by the Supreme Court of the United States: the powers and function of the court would be the same as those presently exercised by the Appellate Committee – subject to some fine tuning to accommodate the hearing of devolution issues which up to now had been heard by the Privy Council. With something of a rhetorical flourish, he said that what he he wanted was a supreme court "severed from the legislature; established as a court in its own right, re-named and appropriately re-housed, properly equipped and resourced and affording facilities for litigants, judges and staff such as, in most countries of the world, are taken for granted."[7]

---

[7] The lecture was later to be quoted on countless occasions. It is reproduced in full in the Appendix

## DERRY IRVINE STANDS HIS GROUND

Both lectures were to be frequently cited by government ministers and other politicians in the course of the parliamentary battles which came to be fought some eighteen months later. But in the short term – at least on the surface – the only reaction of any significance was that in response to a written Parliamentary question in the House of Lords, asking whether the government now "favour[ed] the creation of a supreme court of the United Kingdom, independent of the House of Lords, and if not, why not?", Derry Irvine made it clear that recent events had not caused him to have any second thoughts. "The Government", he stiffly replied, "are of the view that a sufficient case has not been made for the abolition of the Appellate Committee of the House of Lords and its replacement by a separate new supreme court." But then a reminder that these constitutional issues were still very much alive came in the form of an interview in the *Times* of 2 April 2003 with the then Chairman of the Bar, Matthias Kelly QC, and at a hearing of a House of Commons select committee coincidentally on the same day. The Bar chairman was quoted as saying that it was "very difficult to understand why our [highest court] should be a committee of the second house of Parliament"; and that it was time for the Lord Chancellor's role to be "dismantled", in particular his responsibility for judicial appointments. (It was not without significance that, at the time this interview took place, the relationship between the Bar and the Lord Chancellor had become somewhat fractious due to his decision to approve drastic cuts in legal aid, and to suspend the appointment of QCs pending the outcome of a review of the "silks system".) On the very same day on which this *Times* interview appeared,

Lord Irvine, together with his permanent secretary, gave evidence before the newly constituted House of Commons Select Committee on the Lord Chancellor's Department. That hearing is of particular interest in the light of the fact that Lord Irvine was to leave office in somewhat dramatic circumstances just two months later.

He told the Committee that he regretted that because of the many other demands on his time he did not sit as a judge on the Appellate Committee as often as he would like, and that regarded such sitting as an important aspect of the office of Lord Chancellor. He was then asked by the Labour MP James Cunningham: "If you are not able to perform your role as a judge, why do you retain that role.?" Mildly exasperated, he pointed out that he was simply seeking to explain that sitting as a judge was just one aspect of being head of the judiciary: the question was not a matter of how often did he sit but whether he was *entitled* to sit. Rather missing the point of that answer, Mr. Cunningham the persisted in asking: "If you not able to sit, with all due respect, why did you take the job?" Lord Irvine replied that he had difficulty in understanding why the issue of frequency of sitting was of such importance to Mr. Cunningham, and that he had already explained that being head of the judiciary involved doing many other things. Asked about the problem of a potential Article 6 challenge were he to decide to sit in a particular case, Lord Irvine effectively repeated what he had said on previous occasions – "Article 6 is not a means by a side-wind to alter our constitutional arrangements. It merely ensures that there is a fair hearing. I would not sit in any appeal where it could be thought that I represented some governmental interest ...." (He chose to side-step Lord Bingham's point that the *appearance* of independence and impartiality mattered as much as the reality.) When asked about the principle of the separation of powers, he replied that "[w]e are a nation of pragmatists, not theorists, and we go quite frankly for what works."

Inevitably, the arguments for and against a supreme court came up for discussion. Prefacing his question with the comment that he himself was not convinced in his own mind of the need for a separately housed supreme court, the Labour MP Clive Soley asked Lord Irvine why should it not be possible for the Law Lords simply to be confined to their judicial role so that one could "have in effect a supreme court without all the trappings." Derry Irvine acknowledged that this would certainly be possible, but made the point (as he had made on previous occasions) that the report of the Royal Commission had concluded that the Law Lords made a valuable contribution to the work of the House of Lords and had recommended that they should continue to do so. Although he made it clear that he was very much alive to the criticisms made by Lord Steyn in his Oxford lecture, (– whose voice, he pointed out, was but one judicial voice among many) – he went on to say that if a new building was to be provided to house a separate supreme court of architectural merit in the middle of London, "the Lord Chancellor would still be the president of the new supreme court", – a somewhat odd assumption to make in the circumstances. Asked by Ross Cranston, a former Labour Solicitor General, whether a separate supreme court building would provide the Law Lords with better resources such as their own library, Lord Irvine acknowledged that would indeed be the case. However, he went to observe that the reality of the present position was that there was a scarcity of funds, and his priority was the renewal of crumbling court buildings up and down the country, and not the provision of a brand new supreme court.

The subject of judicial appointments also came up. Inevitably so, since a few weeks previously a review which had been commissioned by the Bar Council and had been carried out under the leadership of a former Lord Justice of Appeal, Sir Iain Glidewell, concluded that responsibility for making judicial appointments should be handed to an independent appointments body. Lord Irvine said he had noted Sir Iain Glidewell's opinion, but it was an opinion of a retired judge, and "judges dominate most appointments commissions." He was asked whether it was right that as a senior cabinet minister and close confidante of the Prime Minister someone as "political" as he should be making judicial appointments. The alternative, Lord Irvine replied, would be to outsource this activity to a quango. This would be likely to result in the making of appointments on the basis of compromise rather than strict merit, and the system would be vulnerable to the charge of being "a self-perpetuating oligarchy [of judges]." However, he recognised the strength of the contrary argument, and did not rule out the creation of a judicial appointments commission at some point in the future. (In fact a few weeks later the Lord Chancellor's Department started to prepare a consultation paper on the subject.)

There was one particularly poignant exchange. The Labour MP Keith Vaz asked Lord Irvine what, during his six years in office, he regarded as his greatest achievements. It was for others, he said, to judge what could be said to be his achievements, but what had given him the greatest pleasure was his chairmanship of five cabinet committees,– on constitutional reform, devolution, freedom of information, human rights and House of Lords reform.[8] Evidently, he was completely unaware that his chairmanship of five cabinet committees helped to fuel the many concerns about the tripartite aspects of his office. Perhaps more to the point, this artless candour, and the explicit assumption that were a separate supreme court indeed to materialise, he, as Lord Chancellor, would continue to sit and occasionally preside, showed the complete lack of awareness that his position on the issues of reform of the Lord Chancellorship and the need for a supreme court was seriously at odds with many within the inner circles of Government.

## THE GOVERNMENT'S *VOLTE FACE*

Less than ten weeks later (on the 12th June) there came the surprise announcement from 10 Downing Street, courtesy of the Prime Minister's principal spokesman, that the office of Lord Chancellor had been abolished; that a supreme court would be established; and that a new system for appointing judges would be introduced; that Derry Irvine was retiring from government and would be replaced by Lord Falconer, then a Minister of State in the Home Office,[9] who would be in charge of the new Department for Constitutional Affairs, – formerly the Lord Chancellor's Department, and would not be "discharging any of the judicial functions of the Lord Chancellor." The Cabinet had met earlier that day and had been wholly unaware

---

[8]   It is generally accepted that Lord Irvine's work on devolution issues proved to be critical to the success of the legislation.
[9]   A close and long-standing friend of Tony Blair, he had joined the government back in May 1997 as Solicitor General, coming straight from a successful practice at the Bar. Two years later he was appointed the minister responsible for the Dome.

of what was afoot. However, a cabinet re-shuffle was imminent in any event due to the surprise resignation of the Health Secretary, Alan Milburn, apparently for family reasons. This package of reforms was presented by the spokesman as part of the "process of modernisation". Within 48 hours a clarification had to be issued once it had been fully appreciated that it was simply not feasible to abolish the office of Lord Chancellor with immediate effect: legislation would be required to achieve that end.

The circumstances which both surrounded and explained this government *volte face* has been much commented on. Some of the facts are well known, some rather less so. During the two years preceding the announcement there had been growing dissatisfaction at the heart of government (and not simply on the part of the Home Secretary, David Blunkett) with the performance of the Lord Chancellor's Department, specifically in what was perceived to be its inability to get to grips with failings both within the Criminal Justice system and in the administration of civil justice. The rise in violent crime, and the backlog of both criminal and civil cases – specifically asylum cases, the increasing numbers of which was threatening to overwhelm the system – had risen to the top of the government's agenda for action. Several meetings with Irvine and his officials, initiated by Downing Street to discuss in particular the problem created by the number of asylum applications, ended in stalemate. In his political memoir *The New Machiavelli* (2011) Jonathan Powell, Tony Blair's Chief of Staff, described the Department as "antiquated": at the time, less polite words were often used. The problem lay in the fact that Derry Irvine did not see matters in the same light, and was mainly concerned in keeping David Blunkett's

ambitions in check. In fact two years previously a plan
hatched in Downing Street to transfer responsibility for
the running of the courts in England and Wales from
the Lord Chancellor's Department to the Home Office
(and of course by extension, to the Home Secretary)
had only been thwarted at the last minute by the
intervention of the senior judges, who had been alerted
by Lord Irvine. The Lord Chief Justice, the Master
of the Rolls and the President of the Family Division
went to see Tony Blair to try to persuade him that such
a move would have potentially serious implications
for both the rule of law and the independence of the
judiciary. Their efforts were successful. A remarkable
consequence of this perceived need for secrecy was that
neither the abolition of the office of Lord Chancellor
nor the creation of a supreme court were the subject of
any Cabinet discussion, or even a Cabinet paper.

In due course two of Tony Blair's closest advisers,
Andrew Adonis, then Head of the No. 10 Policy Unit
(later to have a ministerial career and to be created a
life peer), and the then Cabinet Secretary, Sir Andrew
Turnbull, became very much involved in the fate of
the Lord Chancellor's Department and that of the
office of Lord Chancellor itself. Both were critical
of the anomalous tripartite functions of the office,
and of the apparent conflict of interest to which they
gave rise. What in fact triggered the chain of events
immediately leading to the announcement of 12 June
was what occurred in one of several meetings which
Derry Irvine and his Permanent Secretary, Hayden
Phillips attended at Downing Street with Tony Blair
and Andrew Turnbull. To appreciate the relevant
exchange, it is necessary to know that the Lord
Chancellor's Department was housed in Selbourne
House, an anonymous office block in Victoria Street,

whereas the Lord Chancellor and his permanent secretary occupied, rather grand premises in the House of Lords. Irvine was asked by Turnbull (perhaps mischievously) how often did he go to Selbourne House. "I never go to Selbourne House", he replied. Apparently the thought struck both Blair and Turnbull at that moment that a Department of State, with a sizeable and ever-expanding budget, responsible for a wide range of activities within the justice system, surely could not now be run in that way. Furthermore, such a Department of State handling a sizeable budget would be run by an *elected* politician. Andrew Adonis was asked to address the problem.

Although not a lawyer, Adonis happened to have a keen interest in constitutional issues. At Oxford, where for a short period he had held an academic position, constitutional history had been very much his special interest: his doctoral thesis had concerned the political role of the House of Lords between 1885-1914. In regard to the issue of whether there should be a supreme court, he had digested the lectures by Lords Bingham and Steyn, and had kept abreast of other developments such as the reports by the select committees. He produced a paper for Tony Blair which proposed the transformation of the Lord Chancellor's Department into a normal Department of State headed by a cabinet minister, and, as he saw it, the abolition of what would be the redundant office of Lord Chancellor; and the establishing of both a supreme court and of a judicial appointments commission. Quite apart from the "separation of powers" aspect, he saw the removal of the Law Lords from the House of Lords as a logical and important part of the overall reform of the second chamber, and the creation of a supreme court as a symbol of the independence of the judiciary. At the time, as he later explained to the writer, he viewed these changes as "fairly conservative" in the great scheme of things. (Sally Morgan, now Baroness Morgan, and at the time Tony Blair's Political Secretary, recalls that mention of the creation of a supreme court in fact cropped up quite often in discussions among Blair's close advisers about constitutional issues, specifically in the context of reforming the House of Lords.)

All three proposals were strongly supported by both Turnbull and Jonathan Powell, although Powell initially felt that the issue of the supreme court should be separately addressed on a later occasion: in a minute he recorded his view that the supreme court issue "could wait". As far as he was concerned, the immediate and all-important priority was tackling the problem of the Lord Chancellor's Department: this was very much unfinished business.

Tony Blair was persuaded by Adonis's paper and agreed with the proposals. Up to this point he had not showed even the remotest interest in the question whether there was a need for a supreme court, but, as he explained to the writer, he was persuaded that the creation of such court was a logical step once one accepted the premise, which he did, that the fundamental flaw in the office of Lord Chancellor was that it combined an executive/political role with a judicial role. It seemed to him to be "an inescapable conclusion" that the Law Lords, as judges, had by the same token to be separated from the legislature, and therefore removed from the House of Lords. (This of course was a faint echo of the point made by Lord Steyn in his Oxford lecture.)

Ultimately, it was decided to announce all three proposals as a single package of reforms, despite

Powell's reservations. It was thought that this would provide welcome reassurance to the senior judiciary that their independence and the rule of law would not be compromised by the disappearance of the office of Lord Chancellor. Blair and his Downing Street advisers had the concerns expressed on the occasion of the Downing Street visit two years previously very much in mind. [10] Andrew Turnbull thought the news that there would be a supreme court would be greeted by the judiciary "with acclamation." (That thinking would later be reflected in the first contact between the government and the judiciary once the decision to announce the package had been made. The Leader of the House of Lords, Lord Williams of Mostyn QC, phoned the Lord Chief Justice, Lord Woolf, to put him in the picture. His first words were: "I've very good news for you. We are going to have a supreme court." And his next words were: "And we are doing something else. We are getting rid of the Lord Chancellor.")[11]

Despite the fact that Downing Street had other preoccupations at this time, such as whether or not the UK was to join the Euro, It was decided to use the occasion of the next cabinet re-shuffle to make the announcement. Because of Alan Milburn's surprise resignation, the re-shuffle took place sooner than expected. The precise sequence of events was as follows. On the 4th June Hayden Phillips was asked by Turnbull to call round and see him. Turnbull told him what had been decided. Phillips' immediate response was that Derry Irvine should be told, and that it would be best were he to hear it from the Prime

---

[10] This turned out to be something of a misjudgement.
[11] There was an assumption that the views of the Senior Law Lord (Lord Bingham) on the need for a supreme court were shared by the upper echelons of the senior judiciary.

Minister himself. Tony Blair did indeed see Derry Irvine the following day. He told him bluntly that he wanted there to be a supreme court and a judicial appointments commission; and that he had concerns both about the office of the Lord Chancellor and the Lord Chancellor's Department, but without actually spelling out what exactly his own, Derry Irvine's, personal position would be once the changes had been implemented. Irvine saw Tony Blair again a few days later in an unsuccessful attempt to extract more clarity as to what he had in mind.

Derry Irvine and Hayden Phillips then decided that the only way of resolving the issue was to prepare, and send over to the Prime Minister, a minute outlining some of the difficulties about what was being proposed, and explaining in some detail why legislation would be necessary to abolish the office of Lord Chancellor – assuming that option was under serious consideration. (There were, they pointed out, references to the Lord Chancellor and his functions and duties in countless statutes and statutory instruments.) The minute included an offer by Derry Irvine to produce a green paper setting out the proposed package of reforms. The minute was sent over on the 11th June, but – as was apparent from the announcement made the following day – it failed to change the minds of the Prime Minister and his advisers. Their view was that the minute simply reflected Derry Irvine's negative attitude to any of the proposed changes, including the proposed changes to the criminal justice system: in other words, he was part of the problem. The evolving of the plan leading to the 12th June announcement had been shrouded in secrecy and confined to the Prime Minister and a handful of close advisers because it was feared that were the plans to leak out, the senior judges – presumably alerted by Derry Irvine – would prove once again to be obstructive and to cause serious difficulties.

## PICKING UP THE PIECES

It was fortunate that Lord Falconer – "Charlie" Falconer, as he was almost universally and affectionately known by his fellow peers and former colleagues at the Bar – was exceptionally resilient and had a lively sense of humour. He was also extremely astute and had a quick mind. These qualities were to serve him well in the days and months ahead, and particularly when dealing with the more immediate challenges. From a relatively obscure ministerial post in the Home Office he had been catapulted without prior warning into the cabinet and into the newly invented position of Secretary of State for Constitutional Affairs, heading the newly re-branded Department for Constitutional Affairs. A slightly farcical dimension had been injected into his baptism by fire by the recognition within hours of the original Downing Street announcement that (as had been correctly pointed out by Derry Irvine) the office of Lord Chancellor could not simply be abolished by a *fiat* of the Prime Minister. His brief therefore was to pilot legislation through Parliament covering the abolition of the office of Lord Chancellor and the provision of such alternative arrangements as were necessary; the creation of a supreme court; and the creation of a judicial appointments commission. It had already been announced that as interim Lord Chancellor he would not sit in on any appeal in the Appellate Committee, and that he would relinquish the "judicial" role attached to that office.

One of the more immediate challenges confronting him was the need to explain the government's thinking to the Lord Chief Justice, Lord Woolf, and to discuss with him the arrangements which needed to be put in place before and during the passage of the proposed legislation through Parliament. Lord Woolf, like all other senior members of the judiciary, had been taken completely by surprise by the Downing Street announcement. As he later put in an engagingly understated sort of way, he was "not best pleased." He was known for his genial manner and liberal sympathies, and in the event the first conversation between himself and Charlie Falconer within hours of the Downing Street announcement was less awkward than might have been expected. In due course the warm relationship between the two men greatly helped towards achieving swiftly a formal agreement which defined their respective responsibilities (and also dealt with related matters) whilst the proposed legislation was winding its laborious way through Parliament. This was to include recognition of the Lord Chief Justice as the head of the judiciary.

Charlie Falconer was not given any time to "play himself in". Just over a fortnight after having been installed as the Secretary of State for Constitutional Affairs, he found himself giving evidence to the same House of Common select committee which had questioned Derry Irvine in early April. He took the opportunity to confirm that it was the government's intention to introduce legislation to abolish the office of Lord Chancellor, establish a new supreme court and a judicial appointments commission. He said he accepted there were arguments both ways on the need for a supreme court, but thought the need for complete clarity in distinguishing between judicial and legislative functions was a decisive factor. He confirmed his intention not meanwhile to sit in on any appeals to the Appellate Committee. In regard to resources and funding, he acknowledged that the operating cost of the present system of appeals to the Appellate Committee of the House of Lords was virtually self-financing: the receipts from fees largely covering the fairly modest expenditure; and that the funding involved in establishing a new supreme court would require a considerable budget. In response to some persistent questioning, he told the committee that he had been, and continued to be, in total ignorance about what discussions had taken place and what decisions had been made which had led to the departure of his predecessor, Lord Irvine. He reminded the committee that until 12th June he had simply been a Minister of State in the Home Office, and was now doing his best to get to grips with his new job.

Thrown in at the deep end, he clearly was getting to grips with his new job with commendable speed. Under the umbrella of the re-branded Department for Constitutional Affairs, a fifty page consultation paper, entitled *A Supreme Court for the United Kingdom*, was issued just one week after his appearance before the committee, and for which he provided the forward. (Separate consultation papers were issued on the other proposals.) It invited responses on matters of detail, but not on the principle of the proposal itself. In setting out the case for change, the paper quoted from both Lord Bingham's Constitution Unit lecture and from the *Times* interview with the Chairman of the Bar. Its key message was that the establishment of a new supreme court would "put the relationship between the executive, the legislature and the judiciary on a modern footing, which takes account of people's expectations about the independence and transparency of the judicial system." And without expressly acknowledging that it was quoting Lord Bingham, it emphasised the point that in the light of the Human Rights Act, a stricter view had now to be taken not only of anything which might undermine the independence or impartiality of a judicial tribunal, but even of anything which might appear to do so. It rounded off its case for change with on a somewhat portentous note: "The time has come for the UK's highest court to move out from under the shadow of the legislature." The speed with which this consultation paper had been produced was testimony to the "contingency planning" previously undertaken within the former Lord Chancellor's Department.

The paper did not skimp on detail. It drew attention to what it characterised as the cramped conditions and poor resources under which the Law Lords operated under the existing arrangements, and proposed that the administration and funding for the new court would be the responsibility of the Department for Constitutional Affairs. Among other matters it also covered the appointment of members of the new court, the criteria for their selection, the title by which they should be known, whether they should sit as panels or *en banc*, and also the age at which they should retire. The paper made it clear that the Government was open-minded as to the best selection procedure, and the size of the pool from which appointments to the new court should be made. As to title, the government favoured "Justice of the Supreme Court", and had concluded that the members of the court should sit in panels rather than *en banc*. It was open-minded as to whether the retirement age should be 70 or 75. On the other hand the paper made it clear that Law Lords who became part of the new supreme court would be required to sever their connection with the House of Lords, although on retirement they would be free to return to the House and to participate in all its activities.

The consultation process was completed three months later. It came as no surprise that the response to the government's intention to legislate for the creation of a supreme court was distinctly mixed. In the light of that response, and the alarm expressed in some quarters at the proposed abolition of the office of Lord Chancellor[12], what was formerly the House of Commons Committee on the Lord Chancellor's Department and now re-named the Committee on Constitutional Affairs, swung into action once more. The committee held several sessions and heard and received evidence from both serving and retired Law Lords, as well as other senior members of the judiciary. In summarising its conclusions, it reported that it was uniformly agreed that the present system of appeals to the Appellate Committee "worked well [and that] the arguments for change were about principle and perception."; that the proposed supreme court should not be accountable to, or administered by, the Department for Constitutional Affairs; and that the complexity associated with "this bundle of reforms" was such that the government should invite parliamentary scrutiny of the draft proposals before formally introducing any bill.

---

[12]   The Law Lords, although split on the merits of a new supreme court, were united in their concern as to the consequences of the disappearance of the Lord Chancellor. In a formal response they expressed their concern that "that the important constitutional values which the office of Lord Chancellor protected should continue to be protected.... The constitution would be gravely weakened if that safeguard were removed and not replaced."

# PART TWO

# "Purists" versus "Pragmatists": An Arcane Parliamentary Battle

## HOSTILITIES COMMENCE

The report of the select committee served to highlight two central weaknesses of the government's case. The first weakness was that the present system was acknowledged by everyone to work well, and in particular it was universally accepted that the Law Lords were judges of the highest calibre and of undoubted integrity. The second weakness, inevitably to be seen in conjunction with the first, was the considerable cost (both capital and running) which would be incurred in either erecting a new purpose-built building or adapting an existing building to accommodate the new court. It will be recalled that Derry Irvine had made it a familiar refrain that there was a more pressing need to spend money on decaying existing court buildings up and down the country. Charlie Falconer also recognised that the government faced a further difficulty: there was little interest among rank and file Labour MPs in these constitutional issues, and despite Labour having a substantial majority in the House of Commons there were certainly more lawyers within the Tory ranks. Furthermore, there was no one with appropriate experience and expertise to introduce and steer distinctly arcane and complex legislation through the Commons: the attorney general (Peter Goldsmith) like Lord Falconer was a member of the Upper House; and the Minister of State answerable for the Department of Constitutional Affair in the Commons, Christopher Leslie, was not a lawyer. On the other hand, although it was apparent that there would be a significant amount of hostility to the proposed reforms in the House of Lords, one could at least guarantee informed debate and a considerable pool of expertise in that chamber; and, as he later explained to the writer, Charlie Falconer calculated that if the bill successfully negotiated the hurdle of the Lords, it would have a relatively easy passage in the Commons. Therefore, right at the outset, it was decided that the proposed bill would be introduced in the House of Lords, and not in the Commons, although the Opposition had already made it clear that they would oppose it in the Lords.

The government thought it prudent to proceed with caution: Charlie Falconer was only too aware that the speed and suddenness with which the proposals for reform had been brought forward had generated a good deal of hostility and suspicion among the peers, and he realised that the proposed abolition of the office of Lord Chancellor had touched a raw nerve with the judiciary: he recognised that judges saw the Lord Chancellor "as their great protector in government ... a powerful cabinet minister who would privately ... procure the protection of the judges within Cabinet." In any event the drafting of the bill was not yet complete. It was therefore decided first to test the waters by resorting to the tactic of holding what in parliamentary jargon is called a "Take note" debate. This was preceded by Charlie Falconer making a statement the day before, outlining in a little detail what the government had in mind.

Thus it was that on the morning of 12 February 2004, in the words of Hansard, "the Secretary of State for Constitutional Affairs and Lord Chancellor, Lord Falconer of Thoroton, rose to move that this House takes note of Her Majesty's Government's proposals for a United Kingdom Supreme Court, an independent Judicial Appointments Commission and the abolition of the office of Lord Chancellor". He produced a polished performance. He acknowledged that the government's proposals could hardly be said to touch on "bread and butter" issues, but they did concern the "vital issue … [of] the relationship between citizens and the state … and the state includes the judiciary and the judicial system." So far as the proposal for a United Kingdom supreme court was concerned, he declared that this was "another demonstration of [the government's] principles: clarity and transparency in our institutions, and a firm commitment to judicial independence." He quoted Lord Bingham to the effect that it was high time we had a supreme court divorced from the legislature representing constitutional reality, and repeated Lord Bingham's phrase: "Judges are judges, not legislators." He went on to make the point that to "locate our final court of appeal in the Legislature … produces confusion. [This] has led to the Law Lords issuing a self-denying ordinance indicating the circumstances in which they will not speak in this Chamber … on a previous occasion a senior Law Lord was unable to sit on an appeal on which he had commented in the House." (This was a reference to a Law Lord who had both spoken and voted in a debate on fox hunting.) He managed to brush aside a pointed intervention drawing attention to the fact that whilst the government had consulted in respect of the details concerning the creation of a supreme court, it had chosen not to consult on the principle.

Lord Kingsland (in a previous incarnation, leader of the Conservatives in the European Parliament, and at one point in his career – Christopher Prout QC), the shadow Lord Chancellor, replied on behalf the official Opposition. In respect of the supreme court he homed in on the two weaknesses in the government's case: the present system worked well and the cost of replacing it with a new supreme court considerable. "The general public are not foolish.", he pointed out. "They will see that they are getting exactly the same thing for something that is vastly more expensive." He drew attention to Lord Falconer's repeated acknowledgement that "the degree of judicial independence in our courts is beyond reproach; that there is no question whatever that our judges are anything other than completely incorruptible…." He scored a palpable hit when he quoted from a BBC Today programme interview with Lord Falconer, in which, among other things, Lord Falconer was asked: If everything is working so well, why should we change it?", to which he had replied: "It is because it is working so well that now is the ideal moment to change it." "It is a novel legislative proposition", commented Lord Kingsland, "that the better things are working, the more legislation is needed." He also fired a warning shot across the government's bows by endorsing the view of the House of Commons Committee on Constitutional Affairs that draft proposals should be submitted for scrutiny before a bill was formally introduced. (What that meant in practice was submitting the proposals to a House of Lords select committee largely comprising peers with the relevant expertise.)

Lord Lester of Herne Hill responded on behalf of the Liberal Democrats. As one of the key players involved in the submission by *Justice* to the Royal Commission (ante pp. 5-6) he was strongly supportive of the proposals, and explained this at considerable length in a manner that would not have been out of place in the lecture hall rather than a debating chamber. He echoed the view expressed by some (including Lords Bingham and Steyn) that the present appellate system was vulnerable to a successful legal challenge based on Article 6 of the European Convention. His fellow *Justice* campaigner, Lord Alexander of Weedon, who took the Conservative whip, also spoke, but made it clear that he would have preferred the removal of some of the functions of the Lord Chancellor rather than the outright abolition of the office itself. Furthermore, he supported what Lord Kingsland had said on the need for "pre-legislative scrutiny."

Peers of all description spoke in the debate, and contributions from Law Lords, retired Law Lords and distinguished academic lawyers were all much in evidence. Lord Bingham and Lord Steyn chose not to speak (nor to speak in any of the debates which were to follow) because they thought that to do so would compromise their clearly stated position that judges should not be seen to participate in the business of the legislature. The Deputy Senior Law Lord, Lord Nicholls, (greatly respected and admired within the legal profession) had no such qualms. He made very clear his strong opposition to the proposal to replace the existing regime with a supreme court.[13] "The proposal", he said, "is that, lest our [the Law Lords']

---

[13] He had already registered his outright opposition to the notion of a supreme court in an article published in the December 2003 issue of the barristers' "trade" magazine *Counsel*.

continuing membership of your Lordships' House be misunderstood by anyone, we shall all be taken away to a place of safety in our very own judicial ivory tower that will be purpose built or, at least, specially selected." In his view the proposal, although well-intentioned, was misguided: it was unnecessary and do more harm than good. Unnecessary, because "under the present arrangements the Law Lords do not lack independence from the government, nor from the Legislature, and no one suggests that they do." More harm than good, because the Appellate Committee of the House of Lords enjoyed an unrivalled reputation throughout the common law world, and the new court would have to build up a reputation "starting from scratch." He pointed to what would be a less obvious loss. By becoming a member of the House of Lords on his appointment as a Law Lord, he was able to gain a wider perspective by serving on non-judicial committees and attending debates, thereby increasing his awareness "of the broader context in which legislation and policies are formulated." This was in sharp contrast to the "judge-centred" working environment in which he had previously sat as a judge. He finally pointed to the "relatively modest cost" of accommodating the Law Lords in the House of Lords, compared to "the substantial start-up costs and running costs" involved in the creation of a new supreme court.

His colleague, Lord Hoffmann[14], also made his opposition clear. He focused on the curious circumstances in which the government chose to announce its proposals. He clearly enjoyed the opportunity to engage in some less than gentle teasing.

[14] One of the most influential and idiosyncratic Law Lords of recent times.

He began by reminding the House of Lord Irvine's position – *and therefore the government's position* – in regard to the office of the Lord Chancellor and the desirability of a new supreme court, when he, Lord Irvine, gave evidence to the House of Commons select committee less than a year previously, on 2 April. "I have no doubt that, in accordance with the usual practice, it had been cleared with the Prime Minister's office in advance", he commented. "Less than ten weeks later", he continued, Downing Street announced a complete reversal of that position. "It was a remarkable change of policy", he continued, and one carried out with "unseemly haste." Referring to the volatile political context in which this reversal of policy had been announced, he said that "[it] is sad that a great constitutional change should be adopted as a quick fix for personal squabbles in the Cabinet." The specific proposal for the creation of a supreme court, this had emerged "on the coat-tails of the proposal to abolish the office of the Lord Chancellor", Lord Hoffmann drily observed. He endorsed Lord Nicholls' view that there were real advantages in having the House of Lords as a working environment, and that something of value would be lost in a move to a new court. Like others, he saw the issue as one which divided "purists" from "pragmatists". "The distressing feature about the proposal for the Supreme Court", he observed, "is its abandonment of the constitutional pragmatism on which this country has always prided itself, in favour of a sudden enthusiasm for a fundamentalist interpretation of the principle of the separation of the powers. The judicial functions of your Lordships' House are to be rebranded as if they were a commercial product which an advertising agency thought needed to be repackaged and relaunched somewhere else." He added: "And this repackaging comes at some cost."

Another Law Lord, Lord Hope, who somewhat ironically in view of his stance was one day to become Deputy President of the Supreme Court, also spoke. He said he would add only a brief footnote from a personal perspective to what had been previously said by those with reservations about the creation of a supreme court. (It turned out not to be so brief: Lord Hope, as a Law Lord, had many admirable qualities, but brevity was not one of them.) Contrary to what others have suggested, he thought that the existing facilities which the Law Lords enjoyed were perfectly adequate. "It is true", he observed, "that the rooms which we occupy on the Law Lords' corridor lack some of the grandeur of the rooms that are available in the Royal Courts of Justice. We do not have individual toilet facilities, or the individual showers that are provided for some reason to judges in modern court buildings. We do not each have our own secretaries and judicial assistants... in comparison with what we do have, these are trivial disadvantages." But the amenities provided by the House of Lords in other areas, he continued, were of enormous value. He listed as examples, the library, the social contact with lay peers and the opportunity to listen to debates. He found it a wonderful environment, which would not be replicated by a move to another building in another location. Like his colleagues Lords Nicholls and Hoffmann, he referred to the cost involved in implementing the proposal. "If one is searching for value for money and efficiency in cost,", he pointed out, "then the [present] system cannot be bettered."

The retired Law Lord, Lord Lloyd of Berwick, who had previously expressed his strong objections to the proposal of a supreme court to the House of Commons Committee on Constitutional Affairs, weighed in, saying that he agreed with everything Lord Nicholls had said on the subject, and would confine himself simply to making one point. He noted that the Lord Chancellor, echoing Lord Bingham, had emphasised that the Law Lords were judges, not legislators. This line of argument, thought Lord Lloyd, did not get him very far. "The same argument could be made about the many distinguished doctors in the House. They are doctors, not legislators. Who will say that they do not make a valuable contribution to the functions of the House." Lord Lloyd was later to play a significant role in the shaping of the parliamentary battles still to come.[15]

Another retired Law Lord, Lord Ackner, surprisingly chose to launch an attack on what he regarded as the motive behind the proposals for constitutional reform – purely political, he suggested, and dwelt at length on the bizarre circumstances surrounding their original announcement in June of the previous year. He was also critical of the performance to date of the new Lord Chancellor: in a striking passage he observed: "Those of your Lordships who were in the House on Friday 13 June [2003] would have seen the less than suave noble and learned Lord, Lord Falconer, bundling into the Chamber with a full-bottomed wig, clearly borrowed from someone, aware for the first time that he could not leave Parliament to go to his new office without first asking the consent of this House … So the ignorance was there." On the actual merits of the proposal for a supreme court, he confined himself to remarking

[15]  Previously, when giving evidence to the House of Commons Constitutional Affairs Committee, he told the committee: "We have a supreme court in all but name at the moment. Everybody accepts that the Law Lords are completely independent of politics." He went on to say that "the cost of setting up a brand new supreme court [would be] out of all proportion to the non-existent benefit which is a purely theoretical one to do with separation of powers, which I do not accept is a principle of the British constitution."

that although the working conditions in terms of the facilities provided for the Law Lords were rather less than ideal, it did not justify the vast expense which would be incurred in implementing the proposal. His speech displayed an evident hostility which may well have unnerved a less resilient politician than Charlie Falconer.

Lord Millett, on the other hand, who had retired as a Law Lord only in the previous month, took a rather different view both as to the desirability of a supreme court and of the existing working conditions of the Law Lords. He described the Appellate Committee as "probably the worst supported [*de facto*] supreme court of any major jurisdiction in the world." It was precisely because he thought the facilities and working conditions totally inadequate that he supported the proposal for the creation of a new supreme court, but that support was "heavily conditional" on whether suitable accommodation would be found, and was "properly staffed, properly resourced, and properly budgeted with new money, and plenty of it ...."

Lord Brennan, an eminent practising barrister and government supporter, argued that the case for a supreme court was simple and compelling: namely, as pointed out by Lord Bingham, the need to reflect constitutional realities, and the fact that serving judges were not legislators. He said that "these two concepts ... [were] the foundation of the argument in favour of a supreme court" to which he, Lord Brennan, subscribed. "Today's world", he went on to say, "simply does not understand the arguments about the Appellate Committee and the value in the way that Law Lords can participate [in the activities of the House of Lords].... It is said that the system works – that pragmatism is endorsed. I am simply not able to comprehend the constitutional or intellectual concept of pragmatism. It may represent an ability to change where necessary, but it is not an excuse for not changing because some time we might if we need to."

Lord Norton of Louth (a former Professor of Government, and Chairman of the Lords' Select Committee on Constitutional Affairs), who took the Conservative whip, put forward a point of view which had not previously been expressed. "Creating a separate supreme court", he argued, "may have the consequence of isolating the judiciary. Far from protecting the highest court of appeal, I fear that it may make it more vulnerable to attacks from the executive and from Parliament." In his view "the greater awareness on the part of [members of the House of Lords] of the role of the Law Lords .... provides a valuable buffer between the courts and the executive." He described the case for the creation of a supreme court as having "all the characteristics of a lemon meringue pie: superficially attractive but, when you bite it, there is nothing there." He briefly elaborated on this. Alluding to Lords Bingham and Steyn, he explained that "we are told by some Law Lords that the functional separation of judiciary and legislature is a cardinal feature of a modern, liberal, democratic state governed by the rule of law." But in his view, "Either we are already a liberal democratic state governed by the rule of law or we are not. The [view] of some Law Lords implies that we are not. I do not accept that." He seriously questioned whether a challenge to a decision of the House of Lords Appellate Committee based on Article 6 would ever succeed.

He was immediately followed by a former Master of the Rolls, Lord Donaldson, who much regretted that "the senior Law Lord, Lord Bingham, [did] not feel able to put forward his point of view, but instead has to instruct the noble Lord, Lord Brennan to do so."[16] He described the speech of Lord Nicholls as "devastating", and said that he was unable to see what advantages the creation of a supreme court would bring. Pointing out that hardly a single speaker had supported the *totality* of the government's proposals, he said that "the real lesson from this debate is that while the House will indeed take note – it [cannot do] anything else – the person who ought to take note is the noble and learned the Lord Chancellor, and the Government."

There was a characteristically idiosyncratic speech from the irrepressible Earl of Onslow, who in the space of a couple of sentences was able to inform the House what he understood Montesquieu *really* meant by referring to the separation of the powers, and to quote from a Rolf Harris song about "two little boys who had two little toys": the "little boys" he had in mind were the Lord Chancellor and the Prime Minister. His comment on the financial implications of a switch to a supreme court was admirably pithy: "It costs £187,000 to keep the noble and learned Lords in business upstairs. What will the new supreme court cost? Millions." Lord Craig of Radley, a former Marshal of the Royal Air Force, and Convenor of Cross Bench peers, was equally forthright. He observed that "there was not one shred of factual evidence that damns the Appellate Committee. Instead we have a Government trying to bulldoze through a package of constitutional reforms of stupendous import, and contrary to their own strongly expressed views of only a year ago."

---

[16] This prompted Lord Brennan to intervene, and to insist that in fact there had been no contact at all between himself and Lord Bingham in regard to the speech he had proposed to make.

Lord Rees-Mogg, a former editor of the Times and the father of Jacob, also chose to speak, and at some length. He devoted his speech to warning against the danger of falling into the trap of following the example of the United States Supreme Court. His point was that the powers of that court stemmed from the U.S. Bill of Rights, which allowed the court to strike down legislation enacted by Congress. Our own Human Rights Act, he explained, was analogous to their Bill of Rights. "If we have a Supreme Court, already armed with the Human Rights Act", he argued, "we can expect to see the same process here." (Eminent lawyers listening to him were evidently too polite to point out that the Human Rights Act itself expressly excluded such a possibility: section 4 of the Act limits a court's powers, where primary legislation is found to be in breach of the European Convention, to making "a declaration of incompatibility.")

There were speeches from both the Bishop of Chelmsford and the Bishop of Portsmouth. The former alluded to the political origins of the proposal for a supreme court in more measured terms than those expressed by Lords Hoffmann, Ackner and Craig. Referring to the "normal process" associated with such a proposal, namely: "consultation; Green Paper; White Paper and debate", he regretted that "the process which has led to today's debate has lacked that tidy procession." However, he was not against constitutional change, but worried where the pursuit of a separation of powers might take us. The Bishop of Portsmouth said he was simply not persuaded that the proposal for a supreme court [was] worth the effort and the money. He was in favour of "pre-legislative scrutiny."

Lord Goodhart, a distinguished Human Rights lawyer, winding up on behalf of the Liberal Democrats, said he agreed "very strongly with the views of the two noble and learned lords who have not spoken but have made their views clear in public…. They are the noble and learned Lords Bingham and Steyn." He did not support the recommendation of the House of Commons select committee that there should be "pre-legislative scrutiny": the consequence would be that "we would not get the legislation through in this Parliament and who knows who will be Prime Minister or Lord Chancellor in the next [one]."

Winding up on behalf of the Opposition, Lord Henley, the Conservatives' Justice Spokesman, said he subscribed to the "If it ain't broke, don't fix it" school of thought. In respect of the creation of a supreme court the question of whether such move would represent value for money, and more specifically the cost involved, was in his view of central importance. He noted that the Earl of Onslow had suggested that the annual cost of "keeping the Law Lords in this place", excluding their salaries, was £187,000; however, he had heard that the true figure was as low as £160,000. It was vital that the government should provide an estimate of the likely cost of either installing the Law Lords in a new building or adapting an existing one: then a meaningful comparison could be made. He echoed the call for pre-legislative scrutiny.

As Lord Donaldson had pointed out, the flavour of the debate clearly showed that the government were in for a rough ride. Much of the heat generated in the course of the debate, and indeed on which much of the discussion had been focused, centred on the proposal to dispense with the office of Lord Chancellor: in this respect matters had not been helped from the government's point of view by the fact that at this particular time the Asylum and Immigration (Treatment of Claimants) Bill was enduring a stormy passage through Parliament. This was largely because it contained a clause, clause 11, excluding the High Court from exercising jurisdiction to rule on decisions of the Immigration Appeal Tribunal.[17] This was widely regarded within both the legal profession and the senior judiciary as a challenge to the rule of law, and as providing yet another reason why a senior member of the government and cabinet needed to be in place to protect both the rule of law and the interests of the judiciary.[18] Furthermore, the remarkable speed with which these proposals had emerged from the drawing board, – unsurprisingly the subject of a great deal of critical comment in the "Take note" debate, caused widespread irritation. And the sudden death a few months previously of the popular and effective former Leader of the House of Lords, Lord Williams of Mostyn, deprived the government of the services of someone who could have been relied upon to rally much needed support.

What must have been equally concerning was the intervention of the Lord Chief Justice, Lord Woolf. He chose to strike a distinctly cautious, if disapproving, note when giving a public lecture in Cambridge. He had in fact spoken briefly in the Lords debate, but had confined his comments in respect of the proposal for a supreme court to saying that he did not regard it as "a burning issue." His concern on that occasion was to report to the House on the agreement he, on behalf of the judiciary, had reached with Charlie Falconer

---

[17] A somewhat desperate attempt to curb the number of appeals which was threatening to clog up the system.
[18] The clause was subsequently withdrawn.

concerning the arrangements needed to be put in place in the light of the latter's reduced role, and pending the passage of the proposed bill through Parliament. In his Cambridge lecture, which received wide media coverage, he said he was "not wholly hostile to the idea of a new supreme court" but thought that a decision should not be made until a potential building had actually been found, and until one knew whether or not the House of Lords would become an elected chamber. (Reform of the House of Lords was still very much on the government's agenda at this time.) And alluding to the fact that the proposed supreme court would have the same function and powers which the Appellate Committee presently had, – and therefore would not have the power to strike down primary legislation –, he made the tart – and later, much quoted, comment that "among the supreme courts of the world our supreme court, because of its limited role, would be a poor relation. We will be exchanging a first class Final Court of Appeal for a second class Supreme Court." His verdict on the government's proposals was that to "push ahead now, despite the many reservations which have been expressed would be … inconsistent with the desirability of achieving constitutional change by consensus."

## A "WRECKING AMENDMENT"

Despite the inauspicious omens, the government decided to go full steam ahead once the drafting of the bill had been completed: the introduction of the bill had featured prominently in the Queen's speech, and of course had to be referred to, and approved by, the House of Commons. It covered in some detail the functions and duties of the Secretary of State in relation to the judiciary and the rule of law, *absent* a Lord Chancellor; the creation and composition of, and appointments to, the supreme court, and also its powers and procedures; and the creation and composition of a judicial appointments commission. So just four weeks after the "Take note" debate had taken place, the Constitutional Reform Bill was introduced in the House of Lords. Technically, this was a "second reading" of the bill. If things had gone according to plan, the bill, following a lively debate, would then have proceeded to the "Committee stage" for detailed consideration. But things did not go to plan. An ambush had been carefully prepared. Lord Lloyd, the retired Law Lord, who had registered his implacable opposition to the proposals in the "Take note" debate, tabled an amendment to the government's motion to "commit the bill for further consideration" in the usual way by first requiring the bill to be considered by a select committee. He had evidently done his homework. A precedent for taking such a step could be found back in 1975 when the Hare Coursing Bill was committed for scrutiny to a select committee of the House of Lords, never to re-emerge. Presumably Lord Lloyd hoped that the Constitutional Reform Bill would suffer the same fate were the same procedure to be adopted. Furthermore, he had the strong support of the Conservative opposition.

In the ensuing debate, attention was devoted in equal measure to both to the tabled amendment and to the merit of the proposals themselves. A number of peers were eager to speak who had not been present for the "Take note" debate. Lord Falconer did not hold back on what he regarded as the probable effect of the amendment. He made it plain that in his view to accept the amendment would ensure that the bill would never return to the full House for consideration in the present Parliamentary session, and that the Commons would never meanwhile have an opportunity themselves to consider the bill. He pointed out that the proposals had been consulted on in detail for seven months, and "will be debated in Parliament for many months to come. They will receive proper and detailed scrutiny." In the case of "a constitutional change of this importance", he went on, "consideration by the elected Chamber is the foundation of our parliamentary democracy.... To prevent the Commons even looking at this bill is to break with that approach.... The effect of the amendment [tabled] by the noble and learned Lord, Lord Lloyd of Berwick, is that the Bill will certainly not be passed by Parliament within this session, and it may never be considered by the Commons." Referring to the precedent of the Hare Coursing Bill in 1975, he pointed out that "that bill, once referred to a Select Committee in this House, was killed there. The Commons never got a chance to look at it."[19]

Lord Lloyd responded with some spirit. Yes, there had been consultation about the details, but *none* about the principle. And he proceeded to remind Lord Falconer that some two years previously the House of Lords had accepted the recommendation of the then Leader of the House, Lord Williams of Mostyn, that virtually all major bills should as a matter of course be subject to pre-legislative scrutiny. "This bill was therefore an obvious candidate for such scrutiny", he pointed out. Furthermore, since the House of Commons Constitutional Affairs Select Committee

[19] Two peers with long memories who spoke in the debate made the point that the reason the Hare Coursing Bill was "killed" by the select committee was that it was a thoroughly bad bill, –"ill thought out in every way".

had itself advised that there be such scrutiny in this instance, to ignore that advice would be "to show a lack of respect for the other place." He went on to explain ways in which scrutiny by a select committee would help. In regard to the proposal for a supreme court, it could explore the question of cost and clarify what exactly was the cost of "running the House of Lords as a judicial body" and the likely cost of "removing the Law Lords to what the other day was called 'a place of safety'". And the select committee could investigate what exactly was the alleged benefit in establishing a supreme court. In expanding on what he meant by this, Lord Lloyd shamelessly took the opportunity to elaborate on his reasons for objecting to the proposal:

"The only benefit so far identified by the Government is the removal of a so-called perception in the mind of the public: a perception that the Law Lords are not independent; a perception that their decisions are politically motivated; and a perception that they are operating under the shadow of Parliament. Those ... are the words of the Government in their consultation paper. I find it very difficult to take those words seriously .... I have never met anyone with those perceptions and I wonder whether the noble and learned Lord, the Lord Chancellor, has done so .... It may be said that that the Government do not need hard evidence of such perception because it is the job of politicians to know the public mind. So we in this House are being asked to legislate on the basis of a double perception ... we are being asked to legislate on the basis of the Government's perception of a perception in the mind of the public."

Challenged by a peer as to whether he was prepared to take seriously the view of some "distinguished Law Lords" that it was high time we had a final court of appeal which reflected and represented constitutional reality, Lord Lloyd replied that he did indeed take those views seriously, but Lords Bingham and Steyn were what he would call "constitutional purists" whereas he, on the other hand, was "a realist." "I see the cost of making this change and I am trying to compare it with the benefit.", he said. In fact, far from there being any actual benefit, there would, in his view, be a real detriment in removing the Law Lords from the House of Lords for the reasons given by Lords Nicholls, Hope and Hoffmann in the "Take note" debate.

Lord Kingsland, leading again for the official Opposition, made clear his support for Lord Lloyd's amendment, recalling that he himself had previously called for pre-legislative scrutiny. He drew attention to Lord Woolf's Cambridge lecture, drawing attention in particular to Lord Woolf's call for the need to achieve a consensus. Most of his fire was directed to the proposed abolition of the office of Lord Chancellor: he dismissed the proposal of a supreme court as "pointless and extravagant."

Lord Lester, on behalf of the Liberal Democrats, strongly opposed the amendment. Referring the bill to a House of Lords select committee for scrutiny, he said, would have one of two unhappy consequences. The first was that there was a strong probability that the resultant delay would mean that the bill would not be enacted before the next general election (scheduled for Spring 2005). That would mean that the present somewhat imperfect arrangements, resulting from the fact that the Lord Chancellor, having relinquished his role as head of the judiciary but maintaining a role in the making of judicial appointments, would continue indefinitely, and without there being in place adequate protection either of the interests of the judiciary or any adequate safeguarding of the rule of law. The second consequence could be that the government might choose to "withdraw the bill from this House and introduce it in another place. It is a flagship bill to which they are firmly committed." However, his former fellow Justice campaigner, Lord Alexander of Weedon, QC, who had previously in the "Take note" debate regretted the lack of "pre-legislative scrutiny", provided strong and forensically effective support for Lord Lloyd's amendment. He pointed out that there had been no hint of the government's policy on these matters in the previous election manifesto; there had been no prior discussion "with the judges, with the Attorney General, with the leader of our House, with any of those who use legal services or with human rights groups. Nor ... did any Cabinet meeting or the Cabinet itself discuss the issue before the Prime Minister ... announced these changes. So ill-considered was the new policy that the government mistakenly thought they had abolished the office of Lord Chancellor by a combination of Prime Ministerial *fiat* and press release."

The tabling of the amendment provoked a strong reaction on the part of Lord Carter, the government Chief Whip. He had not intended to speak, he said, but had changed his mind on seeing the amendment and listening to Lord Lloyd. The tone was set by his opening remark: "[T]he noble and learned Lord, Lord Lloyd of Berwick, said that as he had spoken on 12 February he intended to truncate his remarks. I cannot help wondering how long he would have spoken for if he had not spoken on 12 February." And before turning to the amendment itself, he thought it right to address the question whether any serving or retired Law Lord should either speak or vote on the amendment. The issue raised by the amendment had clearly become a political one, and the terms of Lord Bingham's statement of June 2000[20] precluded participation by the Law Lords in respect of matters where there was a strong element of political controversy. Retired Law Lords were still eligible to sit judicially, and one must therefore assume that the statement must apply equally to them as well. He noted that Lord Lloyd "had spoken on 36 occasions since June 2000 and had sat judicially 28 times." Lord Carter then turned to the likely consequence were the amendment to be carried. He drew attention to the House of Lords' rules in regard to select committees. These provided that if a select committee considered that a bill should proceed [for further consideration by the full House], and the committee so reports "with such amendments as it sees fit,.. the bill is then recommitted to a Committee of the full House.....If the committee considers that a bill should not proceed, it reports the bill accordingly without amendment." The bill is then not recommitted. "Are the noble and learned Lord, Lord Lloyd of Berwick, and those who support his amendment", demanded Lord Carter, "really proposing that 12 or perhaps 16 members of this House should have the power to recommend that a major constitutional bill should not proceed, or have the power substantially to amend the bill?" His final point was that there had been 440 published responses to the consultation papers, and the evidence to a select committee would in most instances be a repetition of what had already been known and absorbed.

[20] See p. 6 *ante*. The statement had actually been drafted by Lord Bingham's predecessor, Lord Browne-Wilkinson.

Lord Brennan, who, it will be recalled, argued strongly in favour of the government's proposals in the "Take note" debate, took up Lord Carter's point about the undemocratic nature of what would be implied by passing the amendment. "A supreme court separate from the legislature, an independent commission for judicial appointments and the statutory underpinning of the independence of the judiciary are matters of the greatest moment", he declared. "They are matters that should properly occupy debate in the Chamber and the other place, and not in a select committee." The need for an independent appointments commission was generally well recognised and relatively uncontroversial, he pointed out. The arguments for and against a supreme court were well known and had now been rehearsed for some time. The critical question was surely one of principle: are we in favour of it or are we not? "What reason", he asked, does that give for delay? None. It is a matter for this House to decide, if necessary by a vote in this chamber."

Speaking in support of the amendment, Viscount Bledisloe, otherwise known in his working life as Christopher Bathurst QC, and like Lord Brennan a practising barrister, chose to put the boot in,– in no way inhibited by the fact that he was a member of the Lord Chancellor's former chambers. "This bill is thoroughly ill thought out" he declared, "and requires further scrutiny before it comes to the full body of either House": a judgment which was confirmed, he pointed out, by the admission of the Lord Chancellor that further amendments to the bill would be necessary. He noted tartly that the Lord Chancellor had "utterly failed" to answer the question asked by John Humphreys in the Today programme (previously referred in the "Take note" debate): what on earth was the hurry?

Perhaps more ominously from the government's point of view, Lord Neill of Bladen QC, the greatly respected former chairman of the Committee for Standards in Public Life, a grandee of the Bar and former Warden of All Souls, voiced his opposition to a supreme court. (One wonders how many peers present at the debate appreciated the delicious irony that the now celebrated lecture in which Lord Steyn had delivered his telling broadside in support of the case for a supreme court, should have been named in his, Lord Neill's, honour.) "Those who espouse the Supreme Court base their case on an article of faith", he observed: "namely, a belief that judging, legislating and creating or implementing social policy are different activities." He did not believe that was true anymore; he believed the role of the courts and the judges, largely due to the growth in judicial review and the impact of the Human Rights Act, has changed fundamentally during the past fifty years. He also thought the public would lose the benefit of the contribution which Law Lords made to the legislative work in committees of the House, and in debates on law reform. Furthermore, there would be practical difficulties about the new building: there were "two certainties and one probability. The certainties [were] that there [would] be an overrun on cash and an overrun on time – the building [would] be late. The probability [was] that it will be ugly."

Many peers, like Viscount Bledisloe and Lord Neill who had been unable to speak in the previous debate, chose to speak. The veteran Conservative politician Lord Waddington said he couldn't see what practical benefit a new supreme court would bring. "It could turn out to be a very expensive business", he commented. And in a sly dig at Charlie Falconer, he added: "The history of the Dome, after the noble and learned Lord got his hands on it, does not exactly inspire confidence." Lord McCluskie, a former Scottish judge of great distinction, weighed in both on the issue of a new supreme court and the amendment. He praised the work of both serving and retired Law Lords undertaken in various committees of the House of Lords. They did "valuable work ... and it would be a shame to take them away from that precipitously." He went on to say that a "good deal of nonsense has been spoken about separation of powers .... Has the matter suddenly become of such urgency that it cannot be subjected to scrutiny by a select committee? He would, he said, "hate to be accused of sinking a flagship, but {he} certainly would not mind if it were put into dry dock and had its bottom examined by a few experts – just to see whether it was seaworthy."

Baroness Jay, a former Labour Leader of the House of Lords, said that she found "no persuasive argument against the political judgment that the roles of the senior judiciary, Parliament and the executive should be clearly delineated in a modern constitution"; and noted the many anomalies to which Lord Steyn, in his 2002 lecture, had drawn attention. She was impressed by the fact, drawn to the public's attention by an eminent academic lawyer, that nowadays candidate states for membership of the European Union would not be admitted if their judges sat in the legislature. Furthermore, she did not think the House of Lords would be in danger of losing a "legal perspective" were the twelve Law Lords to depart: "I understand", she tartly observed, "that there are about one hundred peers with a legal background among

58

your Lordships."[21] She found the tabled amendment
"very unhelpful." Lord Marsh, a veteran Labour
politician – once upon a time the youngest member
of Harold Wilson's cabinet, described the amendment
in terms which others had simply hinted at as "a
blatant wrecking amendment." It was clear to him
that "key people supporting the amendment [did]
not want the bill to go through." He was immediately
followed by Lord Desai, a government supporter and
distinguished economist, who said he agreed with
"practically everything ... Lord Marsh [had] said."
In his view what was proposed in the bill was long
overdue. It wasn't relevant whether a "nice building"
could be found for the supreme court. "Presumably...
[the judges] could continue where they are now until a
building is provided. If we have to put a different sign
on the doors of Committee Rooms 1 and 2 ... saying
"Supreme Court", that is fine."

Lord Stoddart of Swindon, a veteran Labour
politician with somewhat maverick tendencies, in open
defiance of his party's official line, denounced the bill
as "a piece of constitutional vandalism, undermining
judicial and political relationships built up over the
centuries, and which still worked well." He made
it clear that he was referring both to the abolition of
the office of Lord Chancellor and the removal of the
Law Lords. Lord Morgan, a Welsh historian and
broadcaster, chose to take a swipe at Lord Woolf's jibe
in his Cambridge lecture that what the government
envisaged was "a second class Supreme Court."
Lord Woolf, observed Lord Morgan, instanced "the
fact that it was not based on the American model. I
taught American history for many years and I am

[21] That number, she omitted to point out, included several retired
Law Lords.

extremely glad that it will not be like the Supreme Court of the United States." The Bishop of Worcester provided a novel perspective to the debate about the merits of a supreme court. In his view the concept of the *integrity* of the judiciary was more important and fundamental than the concept of its independence. He had come to the conclusion that separation of powers was no guarantee of that integrity, and he believed that sending the Law Lords to a separate building would not achieve that purpose. "The presence of the Law Lords in this House", he observed, "… is itself a statement about the integrity of our society at the highest level in this land." Earl Ferrers, the doyen of hereditary peers still allowed to sit in the chamber, and a former Conservative minister, was more down to earth in his approach to the proposed removal of the Law Lords. "[T]he hereditary peers have become an endangered species", he lamented, "but we are not alone. Now the Law Lords are to be thrown out .... What on earth has come over the government? What is so wrong with … the judges that they have to be upheaved in this manner? Why do we have to despise and destroy so much of what is good in this country?" In his view the Law Lords "contributed hugely to the formative process by which raw bills are turned into reasonable laws."

Undeterred by the rebuke administered by Lord Carter, three retired Law Lords in addition to Lord Lloyd chose to speak. Lord Ackner returned to the fray. He rejected the notion that the tabled amendment was a wrecking amendment: it was consistent with the government's stated "desire for pre-legislative consideration." Specifically, in regard to the issue of a Supreme Court, a select committee would need to consider who was to pay for the building and its general maintenance; why no provision in the bill had been made in the bill suspending the operation of the proposed court until appropriate accommodation had been found; and lastly, why no cost-benefit analysis had been made. Lord Jauncey, a former Scottish Law Lord, ridiculed the notion that somehow a supreme court would increase and strengthen the judges' independence. He pointed out that the fact that "[he] was working here, writing [his] judgments upstairs in a room, never had the slightest bearing on how [he] decided a case." Lord Brightman, who recalled that he had been appointed a Law Lord some twenty two years ago, thought that replacing the Appellate Committee with a supreme court totally unnecessary. There was already a convention that Law Lords do not speak or vote on matters where there is a strong party political ingredient. All that was needed, he pointed out, was a convention that the Law Lords in office do not speak or vote at all. He could see no benefit to litigants: appeals would not be heard more speedily or more cheaply. So "precisely what [was] the point of sending the Law Lords packing?" He said he had found the working conditions perfectly adequate: the "only small deprivation" was that he no longer had his own personal loo which he had when a High Court judge, but he felt that "that particular deprivation [was] not worth the expenditure of millions of pounds in setting up a supreme court elsewhere."

After the winding up speeches on behalf of the three main parties, it was not until 11.30 in the evening that the House divided. 216 peers voted in favour of the amendment; 183 against: a majority of 33. Of the serving Law Lords, only one, Lord Hoffmann, voted, and did so in favour of the amendment: according to an entry in Lord Hope's diaries, Lord Hoffmann "could not be dissuaded." Lord Irvine also voted: but against the amendment. The bill was thus referred to a select committee of the House for further scrutiny. Following the vote, Baroness Amos, the Leader of the House, adopted an almost funereal tone:–

> "… [T]his House has taken a very serious step. By this vote this … unelected House has made it impossible for the democratically elected House of Commons to receive this bill promised in the Queen's speech in November in time to consider it in this session. That is very serious indeed, and the Government will consider what the consequences may be."

The response of Lord Strathclyde, the Leader of the Opposition, was to observe that the only likely consequence would be that the bill would be carried over into the next Parliamentary session – hardly the end of the world, he implied. Nevertheless, were a bookmaker to have given the odds on the bill ever making it to the statute book – and a Supreme Court building ever seeing the light of day – at that particular moment of time, the odds surely would have been somewhat against.[22]

## A PAUSE IN THE HOSTILITIES

The Select Committee on the Constitutional Reform Bill – to give it its official name – sat down to business

---

[22] It should be mentioned that the Lord Chief Justice, Lord Woolf, spoke briefly in the debate, but only from a position of strict neutrality. His function, he said, was to report the view of the Judges' Council, of which he was chairman. The judges strongly supported the proposal of an independent appointments commission, but had no agreed position on the supreme court proposal: he himself was "ambivalent on the subject."

some three weeks later. The declared sympathies of its sixteen members were evenly divided. Most of them had spoken in one or other of the two debates, including Lord Kingsland, Lord Carter, Lord Goodhart, Lord Lloyd, Viscount Bledisloe, and indeed Lord Falconer himself, who would also double up as a key witness. Its chairman was Lord Richard QC, a former (rather short-lived) Leader of the House, a former UK Representative at the United Nations, and for a time a practising barrister. In its composition the Committee broadly reflected the composition of the House of Lords as a whole in terms of party allegiance: five Labour members, five Conservative members, three Liberal Democrats and three crossbenchers.

Predictably, the Committee received a voluminous amount of written evidence: this included the response previously submitted by the serving Law Lords to the government's consultation on the need for a supreme court, and re-submitted as evidence to the Select Committee. This document frankly acknowledged that the serving Law Lords were evenly divided between those who "on pragmatic grounds believed the proposed change to be unnecessary and... harmful" and those who "regard[ed] the functional separation of the judiciary at all levels from the legislature and the executive as a cardinal feature of a modern democratic state governed by the rule of law."[23] They were also

[23] By the time the Select Committee had swung into action, and after the Law Lords' memorandum had already been submitted as part of the consultation process, two new Law Lords had arrived on the scene to replace two who had meanwhile retired: Lord Brown of Eaton-under-Heywood and Baroness Hale of Richmond. Lord Brown's recollection is that once he had arrived, he had a clear preference for staying put: he liked the ambience – the "buzz" and the gossip in the Palace of Westminster. Lady Hale, on the other hand, who submitted her own written evidence to the Committee, placed on record the fact that her "own support for a supreme court separate from the legislature [had] been reinforced during

divided on the question whether the most senior judicial office holders – such as the President of the Supreme Court and the Lord Chief Justice – if already life peers, should be barred from sitting or voting in the House of Lords; or if not already ennobled at the time of their appointment, should be barred from receiving a life peerage. But they were united on a number of points. The court, they thought, "should enjoy corporate independence" in the sense that it should have its own budget and should not be administered by the Court Service of England and Wales. They were agreed there should be no change in regard to jurisdiction (except for the hearing of devolution issues), and that the total number of Law Lords should continue to be 12, and should continue to sit as panels and not *en banc*. Appointments to the court, they thought, should be made on the recommendation of the proposed Appointments Commission.

Retired Law Lords also submitted written evidence. The shortest and most succinctly expressed came from the long-retired Lord Brightman, who repeated the point which he had made in the second debate that the perceived "separation of powers" problem could simply be solved by introducing a convention that Law Lords should not speak or vote at all in the Chamber. Inevitably, the lengthiest and certainly the most scrutinised memorandum submitted to the Committee came from Lord Falconer, outlining in detail the reasoning behind what was proposed in the bill. In explaining the thinking behind the proposal for a supreme court, he made the telling point (which had only previously been made in passing in the course of the two debates) that the fact that it "became

the three months [she] had spent in the House of Lords. This [was] an intensely political place."

necessary in June 2000 for the Senior Law Lord to make a statement [outlining] the circumstances in which the Law Lords would speak in the House ... reveals in stark form {that] a fault line [was] beginning to open up in our constitutional arrangements..." The memorandum also disclosed detailed estimates of the cost of both setting up and the running of the supreme court, and also disclosed the cost of running the existing Appellate Committee system.

A great deal of the oral evidence heard by the Committee (as was the case with the written evidence) focused on the implications of abolishing the office of Lord Chancellor, and on the functions and status of the secretary of state, but the issue of the supreme court continued to provoke lively exchanges and sharp disagreement. Lord Falconer was pressed by both Viscount Bledisloe and Lord Lloyd on the "perception" point. Had he any evidence that "there [was] a public perception that the Appellate Committee [was] not independent, and if so, [would] it not be better to spend [the] money on correcting that public perception, rather than embarking on this completely new change?" His response was that the argument in favour of a supreme court was that repeated time and time again by the senior Law Lord, Lord Bingham: that our constitutional arrangements should reflect reality, and should be transparently clear to everyone.

He was also pressed on the more immediate practicalities once the bill had become law. Assuming a building ready for immediate occupation could not be found once the Act had come into force, where would the Law Lords (presumably now the Justices) sit in the interim? He acknowledged it was most unlikely that they would move from the House of Lords to one place and then to a permanent Supreme Court building once it was ready. This drew the comment from another member of the Committee that if indeed a supreme court were created, it "would have the same judges as at present, the same jurisdiction and possibly sit in the same building." So, that member continued, did not this show that the reason for the proposed change was indeed perception rather than "any dissatisfaction with the present system?" The present system lacked clarity, Charlie Falconer tersely replied. "The vision [was] of a Supreme Court in a properly appointed building entirely separate from Parliament."

Both Lord Bingham and the Deputy Senior Law Lord, Lord Nicholls, gave evidence to the Committee. In one respect Lord Bingham's views had undergone a change since his *Justice* lecture delivered back in October 2001. This concerned the office of Lord Chancellor. He told the Committee that he had come to the conclusion that no useful purpose was served by the Lord Chancellor sitting in the Appellate Committee, and he doubted whether "someone could be credibly regarded as the head of the judiciary if he was actually not a judge at all." His explanation for reaching that conclusion was compelling. After making the point that during the last three years Lord Irvine was in office, he had sat on only two cases, Lord Bingham explained: "We agreed between us that he couldn't do anything to do with crime because that affected his colleague, the Home Secretary. He couldn't deal with human rights because he piloted the Bill through the House. He couldn't deal with judicial review because it was of governmental interest, and he couldn't deal with commercial cases because they went on for much longer than he could possibly sit." That left him with only two cases on which he could sit: "one about whether premises could be a dwelling for the purposes of the Rent Act if they did not have a kitchen, and one about the construction of a mortgage deed." He said that had he, Lord Bingham, been in the Prime Minister's position in June 2003 (–i.e. at the time of the Downing Street announcement) he would have removed both the judicial function and the Speakership of the House of Lords, but still retained the office of Lord Chancellor.

In respect of his views on the need for a supreme court, however, there was no change. Both he and Lord Nicholls were asked if the experience of the United States Supreme Court suggested there was a danger that a supreme court in the UK would increase its powers particularly in respect of judicial review cases. Lord Nicholls thought there was indeed a danger. Lord Bingham said that he emphatically disagreed. "We have centuries of tradition behind us", he replied. "The bedrock of our constitution is respect for the sovereignty of Parliament .... For my part, I would totally reject the analogy with the United States Supreme Court. Their history is quite different, the origin of their doctrine on the subject ... is quite different ...." Asked whether the title "Supreme Court" might itself encourage something akin to *follie de grandeur*, Lord Bingham simply replied that he could "see no reason why everybody should have a rush of blood to the head as a result of this title ...."[24]

[24] The proposed name to be given to the new court attracted a good deal of discussion during the hearings of the Committee. For instance Lord Mackay of Clashfern, the former Conservative Lord Chancellor, who was opposed to the creation of a supreme court, told the Committee that in his view the title "Supreme Court of the United Kingdom" was misleading: the public would be misled into thinking the court would exercise the same powers as the U.S. Supreme Court; and furthermore the court, as was presently the position with the Appellate Committee, would not have jurisdiction to hear appeals in Scottish criminal cases. He also happened to think one "should take seriously" the fear that the title might influence the conduct and approach of the members of

There were inevitably several lively exchanges between himself and his arch critic, Lord Lloyd. One example will suffice. Putting to Lord Bingham the point he had previously made in the "Take note" debate, Lord Lloyd reminded him of his much-quoted observation that Law Lords are appointed as judges and not legislators, "which", commented Lord Lloyd, "is so true as to be in a sense almost facile." Did that not apply, he asked, to others who are appointed to the Lords – to the doctors, the diplomats and bishops, who have all been appointed because they have reached the top of their professions, and not as legislators? Does not Lord Bingham's view "really ignore the fact that the House of Lords is not just a chamber of the legislature but … a part of the great counsel of the nation where those people should be?" In reply, Lord Bingham said he happened to think that the exercise of the judicial function was a unique function. "That is not to say that it is a better job than anybody else's – one does not need to get into childish arguments of that kind, but it is a different job." This was demonstrated by the fact that a Law Lord could say something in a debate which could disqualify him from hearing a case, or lead to objections being raised to his hearing a case: this had actually happened from time to time.

Commenting on Lord Bingham's reply to Lord Lloyd's question, Lord Nicholls thought that the problem identified by Lord Bingham was obviously one inherent in being a judge functioning at *any* level, and not just being a Law Lord and as such a member of the House of Lords. "This was a perennial danger for judges about which judges have to be on their guard." There were cases where judges had to disqualify

the court.

themselves from sitting on sitting as a result of what they have said in another context on another occasion. He did not regard the risk in the case of the Law Lords as a significant factor in the weighing up of the pros and cons of creating a supreme court. Lord Nicholls was in turn pressed on his repeatedly expressed view that the Law Lords benefited from their social inter-action with the other members of the House of Lords, which his retired former colleague, Lord Nolan, had described as the "wider world." He conceded that he himself would not have described them quite in those terms.

Lord Woolf, the Lord Chief Justice, explained in some detail to the Committee the concerns of the judiciary in regard to the proposed abolition of the office of Lord Chancellor, but declined to express any view on the prospect of a supreme court, which, as he had pointed out in the second House of Lords debate, he did not regard as particularly urgent. Lord Hope, on the other hand, was not so reticent. He submitted a trenchantly expressed memorandum of his own which preceded his oral evidence. Its flavour can be caught from the following extract:

> "The Government, basing itself repeatedly on pronouncements by Lord Bingham and Lord Steyn, has stated that it approaches the establishment of a supreme court for the United Kingdom as an issue of principle. The principle which it asserts is separation between the roles of judges and those of legislators. It adopts Lord Bingham's recent statement that he had yet to hear any principled argument to the contrary…. Lord Bingham and Lord Steyn are of course entitled to their own views of the matter. But they are not the source of all wisdom on these

issues…. The fundamental principle which lies at the root of the rule in the United Kingdom is the independence of the judiciary: [not separation of powers] which is a different principle…. If a principled argument against separation is needed, it can be expressed in the phrases "value for money" and "holding on to what is good."[25]

He went on to reject the suggestion that a Law Lord could be "lobbied" in the corridors of Parliament, something he had never experienced during his seven and a half years as a Law Lord. He stated his belief that it was open to him "to contribute to the work of the House as a revising chamber by drawing attention to possible defects in draft legislation", and pointed out that he had done so on eight occasions. He also drew attention to the valuable contribution which the Law Lords made to work in committees. When it came to his actual appearance before the Committee, however, he was mainly questioned on the Scottish dimension to the creation of a supreme court; the kind of extra-curricular work which he undertook in the House of Lords, and how, if a supreme court were to be established, he saw it could best secure its financial independence. He was not given the opportunity, however, to elaborate on the reasons which he had

---

[25] Like Lord Hope, Sir Robert Carnwath, then a Court of Appeal judge and now a Justice of the Supreme Court, in written evidence to the Committee, rejected the relevance of the "separation of powers" principle: in his view the fundamental principle of the British Constitution was the supremacy of Parliament. And he regarded the reliance placed by critics of the existing arrangements on Article 6 of the European Convention as misplaced. "The European Court of Human Rights", he submitted, "does not insist on a rigid division of functions between the judges and the legislature. It is concerned with specific connections in individual cases."

given in his memorandum for his opposition to the creation of a supreme court.

Of the very few non-lawyers who gave evidence to the Committee, pride of place must go to Lord Rees-Mogg, who evidently felt compelled to reprise his unexpected contribution in the "Take note" debate, albeit at considerably greater length. Reading from a prepared text, he treated the Committee to a closely argued and somewhat densely worded dissertation on the "politicisation" of the U.S. Supreme Court, and on a similar danger which could await a United Kingdom supreme court. This drew from a presumably mildly bemused Chairman, Lord Richard, the response: "... [F]or the life of me I do not see how, if what you are doing is moving the Law Lords out of the legislature into a separate building and giving them exactly the same powers in the new building that they have got up here at this moment ... that should suddenly turn them into a constitutional court ... doing what you do not like the [United States] Supreme Court doing."

In the course of the Committee's many sittings, questions had been asked (as we have seen was the case with Lord Falconer) as to what exactly would happen in respect of the supreme court project once the Constitutional Reform Act had come into force and before the court could be up and running; and precisely what kind of building and accommodation were envisaged. No clear picture had emerged from the answers that had been given. In fact by the time the Select Committee had begun to sit to hear evidence, and although no final decision had yet been reached, all the indications were that the government had earmarked the Middlesex Guildhall, the rather grimy unloved Neo-Gothic building (circa 1912) on the north side of Parliament Square, (then functioning as the Middlesex

Crown Court and comprising seven courtrooms), as the intended location of the new court. It had been realised quite early on that the cost of a new building on a suitably prestigious site in central London would be both unacceptable and unaffordable and would certainly have attracted universal hostility. The "New Wing" of Somerset House (in the Strand) was under consideration as a viable alternative to the Guildhall, but was soon to be rejected for a variety of reasons.

A few days after he had appeared before the Committee, Lord Bingham submitted a memorandum to the Committee, which, in the words of the Committee's eventual report, "reflected the consensus of opinion among the Law Lords" in regard to both questions, and was presumably intended to leave the government in no doubt as to where they stood. It carefully explained why in their view all the existing furniture and fittings in the Middlesex Guildhall would have to be removed and why drastic reorganisation of the space within the building would be necessary. The nature and configuration of the courtroom in a new supreme court complex would have to reflect the fact that appeals (as was presently the case with the Appellate Committee of the House of Lords) would involve difficult issues of law, resolved "by reasoned debate, conducted almost conversationally", the advocacy employed being "far less openly adversarial "in manner than in ordinary litigation. The traditional configuration of the courtroom, with raised bench for the judge and advocates' benches below – plus a witness box, would be "inappropriate and counter-productive." It would also be necessary "substantially to lighten and brighten the present dark and forbidding aspect of the [existing] courts which, however appropriate for a criminal court in 1912, is entirely unsuited to the work we do...." Finally, came the warning shot fired across the government's bows that they, the Law Lords, had "grave doubts whether, even if radically transformed, the space {for the proposed courtrooms] could ever provide a suitable setting [for the new court].... With Parliament Square and the Palace of Westminster to the east, and with Westminster Abbey to the south, the Guildhall site in our view deserves a building very much more distinguished than the Guildhall is or ever can be. The impression will always remain that the Supreme Court has been crudely thrust into a building designed and built for another purpose."

As to the position once the Act has come into force, they accepted that a period of a few years delay would be necessary before the new court would be accommodated. In their view the delay would present no practical difficulty if the Appellate Committee continued to function as it now did. However, "an intolerable situation would arise if the new arrangements were to take effect before there was accommodation to which the judges could transfer." This was because "old" appointees would continue to be peers, and as such entitled to the facilities of the House, and "new" appointees would not be so entitled, unless they were already peers. In their view it was essential that new legislation creating a supreme court should not come into effect until accommodation was available in which the court could function.

In the event the worst fears of some of the bill's supporters proved unfounded. The Select Committee did not "kill" the bill, though it produced a great number of amendments, all of which were accepted by the government. However, the Committee was divided both on the issue of whether the Appellate Committee of the House of Lords should be replaced by a Supreme

Court of the United Kingdom and on the issue whether commencement of the relevant provisions (in Part 2 of the bill) should be delayed pending an actual move to permanent accommodation. The Committee therefore made no recommendation in respect of either issue. They were agreed, however, that the name "Supreme Court of the United Kingdom" and the title "Justice of the Supreme Court" would be appropriate; that the number of Justices should be twelve; and that they should sit in panels and not *en banc*. (The Committee also failed to agree on the question whether the office of Lord Chancellor should be retained, notwithstanding its reduced role and status. Again, it therefore made no recommendation.)

It was hardly surprising that the Committee was unable to agree on the prospect of a supreme court. Nothing new had emerged from the evidence likely to have changed anyone's minds: it is evident from the Committee's report that in fact none of the evidence which had been submitted to it resulted in any change of position on the part of any of its members. As had been confidently predicted by some of those who had argued in the "second reading" debate against referring the bill to a select committee, the evidence largely reflected what had already be set out in written responses to the original consultation paper. It had always been clear that opposition to a supreme court was based essentially on two lines of argument: that the problem was simply one of perception – namely, the mistaken view allegedly held by some members of the public that the Law Lords were part of, and not independent of, government; and that what had been identified as a fault line in our constitutional arrangements, (– the apparent blurring of the division between the judiciary and the legislature) was simply a minor wrinkle, and that the cost of ironing it out in the form of creating a supreme court would be wholly disproportionate: why spend an enormous sum of money on replacing an appellate system which was acknowledged to function perfectly well.

## HOSTILITIES ARE RESUMED

The ensuing scenario could have been worse from the government's point of view: some four months after the previous debate, the bill, albeit heavily amended, returned to the floor of the House, to start formally its passage through the conventional committee stages of the parliamentary process. However, it was soon evident that the passage would prove to be far from smooth. The fate of the office of Lord Chancellor continued to generate a great deal of heat. The degree of sentimental attachment shown to this demonstrably anachronistic office of state could presumably be explained by their Lordships being gripped by the proverbial "heavy hand of history." Lord Kingsland, on behalf of the Opposition, tabled a further amendment to the bill, the effect of which, if carried, would be to secure the retention of that office.

He argued that although there was now a consensus that it was inappropriate for a Lord Chancellor to sit as a judge or perform the role of head of the judiciary, and that in future judicial appointments should be made by an independent commission, there was still a need for a person of standing and "clout" and with a legal background to act as a guarantor of the rule of law, and to safeguard the independence of the judiciary. He was strongly supported by Lord Lloyd and other peers who had been prominent speakers in the previous debates and had served on the Select Committee, including

Lord Howe, the former Sir Geoffrey Howe, former Chancellor of the Exchequer and Foreign Secretary in the Thatcher Government, and one time Solicitor General, who made an eloquent plea for the retention of the Lord Chancellor as a member of the House of Lords: lawyers of standing could no longer be found in the House of Commons, he lamented.

Opposing the amendment, Lord Brennan pointed out that there was no constitutional principle requiring the Lord Chancellor to protect the independence of the judiciary either in Cabinet or otherwise, and that such role could now be more effectively performed by the Lord Chief Justice as head of the judiciary. Winding up for the government, Charlie Falconer argued that once one had stripped the office of Lord Chancellor of the judicial function, the responsibility for making judicial appointments, and the Speakership of the House of Lords, one was left with the purely ministerial/political role of heading a Department of State responsible for a budget of £3 billion. The office of Lord Chancellor would be wholly redundant. Lord Kingsland's amendment, however, carried the day by a majority of 32. Was this a foretaste of the turbulent waters which the government's supreme court project would have to navigate before the committee stage of the bill was completed?

The answer to that question had to wait until the House resumed its committee stage sittings on the bill following the summer recess. Once again, the indefatigable Lord Lloyd took centre stage. He and a few other peers tabled amendments designed to kill the Supreme Court project stone dead. He marshalled the familiar arguments against the project in an impressive manner. We did not need a supreme court to protect and enhance the independence of the highest court in the land: everyone accepted that the Law Lords are completely independent, and one would not add to their independence by moving them to another location. The government had not produced a shred of evidence to support the assertion that the public believed otherwise or that the decisions of the Law Lords were politically motivated. Yes, the Law Lords were appointed as judges and not legislators, but that was true of the doctors, diplomats, Cabinet Secretaries, service chiefs and men of science who are appointed to the House of Lords: they are appointed because they have reached the top of their professions. As to the possibility that the public could be confused by the fact that the Law Lords performed their judicial function in the House of Lords, the public would be much more confused by the creation of a supreme court: they would immediately think in terms of the Supreme Court of the United States. The answer to the argument that the principle of separation of powers requires the judiciary to be visibly separate from the legislature was that there was no such principle underlining our constitutional arrangements. Finally, the notion that Article 6 of the European Convention likewise required a clear separation of the judiciary from the legislature was a wholly mistaken one in the light of recent decisions of the European Court of Human Rights. For good measure, he pointed out that the cost of re-building the inside" of the Middlesex Guildhall, were it to be the chosen site, would be prohibitive.

Lord Goodhart, for one, was not impressed by the force of Lord Lloyd's advocacy. "It is an inexcusable anomaly", he declared, "that in the 21st century the highest court in the land is not a free-standing supreme court but is one of the [two] Houses of the legislature."

Furthermore, in his experience the present system *was* indeed a cause of confusion in the public's mind. He instanced the need for a BBC newsreader, when recently reporting that the House of Lords was about to start hearing the appeal brought by detainees held in Belmarsh prison, that the appeal was being heard by the Law Lords and *not* by the entire House of Lords. He, Lord Goodhart, also deplored the difficulty of access to hearings of the Appellate Committee, an inconvenience shared by practitioners and the public alike. For good measure he added that having once appeared as counsel in an appeal hearing in the chamber of the House of Lords, he could say with confidence that "it was by some distance the most inconvenient court in which I have ever appeared."

Charlie Falconer responded to the case put by Lord Lloyd in an equally succinct manner. "Two principles", he argued, "underpin the government's proposals for a United Kingdom Supreme Court. The first is the functional separation of the judiciary from the legislature. The second is the important need for greater constitutional clarity and visible independence for the United Kingdom's highest court …. The current arrangements simply [did] not meet the expectations of a modern 21st century democracy." He went on to confirm that a final decision as to the chosen site for the supreme court had not yet been made, and he conceded that up to date information as to the chosen premises and as to the likely costing was necessary before the House reached a conclusion. In the light of that concession, the obstructive amendments were withdrawn, and the bill duly proceeded to the "report" stage.

Battle recommenced some two months later. The fate of the office of Lord Chancellor continued to generate some heat, and an amendment tabled by Lord Lloyd requiring the Lord Chancellor to be a member of the House of Lords and *not* the House of Commons was carried by a majority of 23. Another amendment tabled by the Opposition, requiring the Lord Chancellor to be a lawyer, was carried by a majority of 40. And whilst further debate on the fate of the supreme court had still to await the promised up-to-date information from Lord Falconer, there was a significant contribution from the Lord Chief Justice, Lord Woolf, on the subject. In using the occasion to convey the views of the Judges' Council on the bill taken as a whole,[26] he admitted to having undergone a change of mind. He said that although in the past he had not exactly been vocal in his support of a supreme court, he had now come to recognise that "it would have very real advantages over the Appellate Committee". He gave three reasons: it would be more in line with separation of powers; it would be more accessible to the public; and its role would be more understandable to the public. His previous "coolness" had been primarily based on financial considerations: namely, a concern that money would be taken away from maintaining existing courts. Provided the court would be housed in a suitably prestigious building, and resources were made available "without prejudicing the "existing overstretched court budget", he declared, "[then] the creation of a supreme court will have my support and that of the Judges' Council." In his view "the Bill marked a gigantic step forward in our constitutional

---

[26] He reported that the Council warmly supported the bill in its amended form, and that it welcomed the retention of the office of Lord Chancellor but did not think it vital that the office holder should be a member of the House of Lords. As previously mentioned, it had also welcomed the creation of a judicial appointments commission.

arrangements." It became apparent when the debate was resumed one week later, that this unexpected support for the project from both the Lord Chief Justice of the day and the Judges' Council had evidently had no little impact.

Lord Lloyd had tabled an amendment of ingenious simplicity designed to torpedo the prospect of a supreme court in a location separate from the House of Lords. It is worth quoting in full: "The House of Lords, when exercising its appellate jurisdiction, is the Supreme Court of the United Kingdom and the Lords of Appeal in Ordinary shall be appointed in accordance with the provisions of sections 16 to 22." Speaking in support of his amendment, he made it clear he was unhappy about Lord Woolf's change of mind: he sought to rebut each of the three reasons Lord Woolf had instanced for having done so; and was at pains to minimise the weight to be attached to the views of the Judges Council on the matter: "With the exception of the Lord Chief Justice and the Master of the Rolls, the members of the Judges' Council can have little idea of what the work of the Law Lords actually involves. They do not know how very different the work of a Law Lord is from the work of a Lord Justice of Appeal, and from that of High Court judges ...." Nor did they know, he continued, how the Law Lords benefited judicially from being members of the House of Lords, as had been explained by Lord Nicholls in the "Take note" debate. He had clearly been stung by Lord Woolf's intervention, knowing the impact it would have on fellow peers. Not often, one suspects, had the members of the Judges' Council been patronised with such lofty disdain. Lord Lloyd was also cross about another matter: the promised details as to the choice of site for the new court.

Shortly before the start of the resumed debate, Lord Falconer had produced, in the form of a written statement, the promised information as to both choice of site and estimated cost, in which he confirmed that the Middlesex Guildhall was indeed the "preferred choice" – subject to the obtaining of planning consent, and agreement with English Heritage. The proposals "for this self-contained and dedicated building" would include "three large hearing rooms", "greatly improved public access", "an education suite", "the possibility of a live feed from the hearing rooms", a "world class law library" and fourteen "large en suite judicial chambers." He disclosed that the estimated cost of converting the existing building into a "fit for purpose" supreme court would be £30 million.[27] (A breakdown of this sum was helpfully provided.) The estimated annual running costs of the new court, once established, would be £8.8 million: again, a breakdown was provided. There were a number of imponderables, and some figures had still to be provided. He acknowledged that "the Law Lords [had] continuing reservations as to the suitability of this building to house the Supreme Court of the United Kingdom", and gave an assurance that he would "continue to consult with them closely on the issues." Lord Lloyd deplored both the lack of opportunity to study the figures which had been disclosed in the statement, and the omission of figures still required in order to complete the picture. "The decision that we are asked to take", he declared, "involves weighing the alleged merits of creating a Supreme Court and removing the Law Lords against the cost of doing so. How can we

[27] This did not include the cost of relocating the criminal courts then housed within the building: this was costed at an additional £15 million.

make a responsible decision about that without having had a better chance to study all the figures? ... That is why we cannot reach such a decision today ...." The Opposition supported his position, and he eventually withdrew his amendment.

The sharp division of opinion persisted throughout the debate. Lord Howe, who had tabled an amendment linked to that tabled by Lord Lloyd, explained that one of the charming aspects of the Appellate Committee was that it was *not* housed in some grand self-contained building, and that its proceedings had a pleasing informality. There was a good deal to be said for "preserving continuity in maintaining that modesty": locating the new Supreme Court within the Palace of Westminster would ensure this would happen. Furthermore, the Law Lords should retain the style and title of Lords of Appeal in ordinary, and continued membership of the House. Rules or conventions could be introduced if necessary to preventing their speaking in debates or voting. Lord Goodhart took the opportunity to inject a note of harsh reality into the discussion of the role the Law Lords play in the affairs of the House, and the nature of their contribution. Lord Goodhart pointed out the only official role of serving Law Lords in the business of the House is that two of them serve as members of the Committee for Privileges "which hardly ever meets"; and one Law Lord is "the chairman of Sub-Committee E of the Select Committee on the European Union." "It is true", Lord Goodhart continued, "that some Law Lords wish to remain here. Your Lordships' House is indeed a very pleasant and beguiling place, and no doubt many Law Lords enjoy being here"; but it was hard to see how membership of the House benefitted them in their judicial role. In his view it was incomparably a greater distinction to be one of twelve Justices of the Supreme Court. And "it was wrong that the judges of the highest court in the land should have to hear cases perching in two of the Committee Rooms of your Lordships' House and not in their own court building." And it was wrong "that they should have pokey rooms in the Law Lords Corridor rather than proper offices of their own."

There was a measure of agreement on other issues, however. Charlie Falconer made it clear that the government agreed to the inclusion of a "sunrise" clause: in other words, the provisions in the bill relating to the Supreme Court would not come into force until it had been accommodated in "a suitable home". This meant, he said, "that until the new Supreme Court [came] into being, the [Appellate] Committee of the House of Lords [would] continue as before ... [and] all its members [would] be members of this House, with all existing rights." Furthermore, the proposed accommodation would have to be in accordance with plans approved *both* by the Secretary of State *and* by the Law Lords.

The curtain finally came down on this seemingly interminable wrangling over the Constitutional Reform Bill some six days later, when the issue of whether or not there was to be a Supreme Court would be finally resolved – at least in the House of Lords. It was the Third Reading of the bill, and five days before Christmas (2004) and some eighteen months since the famous – or infamous – Downing Street announcement. Lord Lloyd's amendment had been resurrected, and he opened the ensuing debate. It called for, and in fact got, a bravura performance: after all, he now had to contend with the Lord Chief Justice as well as the Senior Law Lord. He seized on one of Lord Woolf's three reasons for supporting the creation of a supreme court: namely, that it would make the role of the Law Lords more understandable. What more do we want the public to understand? he demanded. The day after the near unanimous decision of the Law Lords in the Belmarsh case the previous week, he had looked at the daily newspapers in the Library: they had all covered the story. Most had referred to the Law Lords as being the highest court in the land. "Thus the *Mirror* said "the Law Lords, the United Kingdom's highest court, blows a hole … in the Government's war on terror"; and the *Sun* said "On day one of his new job, the Home Secretary, Charles Clarke, finds out exactly what he is up against." "Surely", Lord Lloyd exclaimed, "any reader of the *Sun* or the *Mirror* would realise that the Law Lords, the highest court in the land, had done something that the Government did not like. How then can it be said that there is confusion in the minds of the public?"[28] Reminded by a peer that the Select Committee had in fact heard some evidence of such confusion, he responded tartly: "[T]wo pieces of evidence were given to the Select Committee. Both were anecdotal. One was given by … Lord Bingham, the other by Professor Diana Woodhouse, who had asked one of her students which was the highest court in the land, and the student had answered that it was the Court of Appeal …. If that is the best evidence that the Government can produce, heaven help us."

In support of Lord Lloyd's amendment, the Deputy Senior Law Lord, Lord Nicholls, returned to the action, commenting in passing that as he was due to retire long before there would be any prospect of a supreme

[28] Lord Goodhart, however, drew the opposite conclusion from the public response to the Belmarsh decision. He told the House that when he appeared on a TV programme on the subject, a viewer phoned in to ask whether in the light of that decision the House of Lords would be abolished.

court actually springing into existence, his views on the subject should be regarded as being entirely objective. On the point as to confusion in the public mind, he drew the same conclusion from the response to the decision of the Law Lords in the Belmarsh case as did Lord Lloyd. Otherwise his speech covered familiar ground – except in one respect. He questioned whether there was any real advantage in exchanging Committee Rooms 1 and 2, in which the hearings of the Appellate Committee were currently held, for specially designed courtrooms in another building. The hearings in Committee Rooms 1 and 2 were relatively informal: the Law Lords sat around a horseshoe-shaped table at the same floor level as the advocates, unrobed; and they had now made it absolutely clear that it was their unanimous wish to copy and reproduce the existing committee room layout and procedure in the new supreme court. Increased sitting capacity for the public was hardly a critical factor: the public appetite for "watching and listening to seemingly interminable legal argument" was very limited. In his experience, most visitors left after a few minutes. Should a case attract an exceptional degree of public interest, then, as had happened in the past, a larger room could always be made available by the authorities. For good measure he also had strong reservations about the suitability of the Middlesex Guildhall as the designated building. He was particularly scathing about some of the interior features which, he understood, were likely to be retained despite the intended wholesale transformation of the building.

Lord Richard, who, it will be recalled, chaired the Select Committee hearings, chose to follow the example of Lord Goodhart in the earlier debate, in questioning the extent of the Law Lords' contribution to the business of the House. "It is not the Law Lords", he observed, "who make the contribution but the *retired* Law Lords." He noticed the presence of more than just a sprinkling of retired Law Lords present in the chamber, and noted that there is "a fair and extremely valuable sprinkling of retired Law Lords" sitting on the many committees of the House.

In winding up for the government, Charlie Falconer chose not to dwell once again on the principles underlying the case for a supreme court – "the arguments are well-known", he observed with masterly understatement,– but to focus on practicalities such as the need for better accommodation. He cited the critical comments of Lord Bingham on the inadequate facilities currently available to the Law Lords. This brought about a sharp and somewhat unseemly exchange about Lord Bingham's views of the Middlesex Guildhall as the preferred site for the new court. Lord Falconer "strenuously disputed" that, as stated by one peer, Lord Bingham "was totally opposed" to the choice of the Middlesex Guildhall. He was then reminded sharply by Lord Lloyd of the memorandum submitted by Lord Bingham to the Select Committee. His response was that though Lord Bingham "had reservations about the building, he did not take the position of saying that it could never be a Supreme Court … he is prepared to talk them [i.e. his reservations] through and see whether changes can be made." The amendment was defeated by 60 votes: a comfortable majority;[29] next it would be the turn of House of Commons.

[29] Also, what was described as "a halfway house" amendment, requiring the Supreme Court to be located with a separate entrance within the Palace of Westminster, had been tabled by Lord Kingsland and Lord Howe: this too was defeated.

Looking back at those House of Lords debates and the travails of the Select Committee, one is struck by three facts. One, although the Conservative opposition had treated, and opposed, the bill as a party issue, much of the running in the resisting of both the abolition of the office of Lord Chancellor and the creation of a supreme court had come from a retired Law Lord, then in his late seventies. Two, but for the tact, patience and general amiability consistently shown by Charlie Falconer in fighting the government's corner, the outcome may have been very different. (His cordial relationship with Lord Woolf may well have played a part in the latter's later conversion to the cause in regard to the supreme court.) And three, whilst the sentimental attachment shown by many peers to the historic and indeed unique office of Lord Chancellor was not very surprising, the passion and degree of interest roused among a sizeable cross-section of peers by the fate of the Appellate Committee and its members, certainly was. One must never under-estimate the effect of the grip of the proverbial "heavy hand of history" on those who conduct their working or public lives within the warm embrace of our institutions.

## THE COMMONS TAKES OVER

The bill arrived on the floor of the House of Commons the following month: (January 2005). The government were in a hurry: they wanted the bill to have completed its passage through Parliament before the next General Election loomed on the horizon – widely assumed (quite correctly, as it happened) to take place in May. Their business managers initially tried to limit the time for debate, but later relented. In the event, the debate (both on the floor of the house and then in Committee) was spread over nearly three days. A great deal of the time was taken up with discussion of the requirements of the office of Lord Chancellor, and both the current and the proposed system of making judicial appointments. The overall tone was rather different from that in the House of Lords.

Although the majority of those who took part were barristers or solicitors, the responsibility for introducing the bill on behalf of the government fell to a non-lawyer, Christopher Leslie, who then occupied the position of Parliamentary Under-Secretary of State for Constitutional Affairs. (More recently he was to acquire an equally modest degree of fame by defecting from the Labour Party to Change UK over the issue of Brexit.) He took the opportunity to capitalise on Lord Woolf's recent conversion, and the rigorous scrutiny to which the bill had been subjected elsewhere: "The Lord Chief Justice and members of the senior judiciary", he pointed out, "support the Government, and a Select Committee of the House of Lords has meticulously scrutinised the bill." When challenged with quotations from certain Law Lords (such as Lord Nicholls) and retired Law Lords as to the adequacy of their accommodation and working facilities, he was able to come up with contradictory quotations from others. He fended off valiantly awkward questions about the necessity or otherwise for the Lord Chancellor in his new role having a legal qualification, and one rather unexpected question from Edward Garnier, a practising QC and later to become a Conservative Solicitor-General, demanding to know why Lord Falconer – "the Lord Chancellor for the transitional period, as he likes to call himself" – saw fit to appoint his former Pupil Master (Lord Justice Potter) as president of the Family Division.

The Conservatives mounted what turned out to be distinctly fierce opposition to the provisions concerning the Supreme Court, led by Dominic Grieve, later to become Attorney-General in David Cameron's coalition government and more recently to play a central role in the twists and turns of the Westminster Brexit drama. He tabled a motion which managed to encapsulate the entirety of the case that had been argued in the House of Lords over the previous year for opposing the creation of a supreme court. He begged to move that: "This House declines to give the Constitutional Reform Bill a second reading because it creates a costly and unnecessary Supreme Court exercising the same functions as the current Law Lords; is based on the false premise that the separation of powers between the judiciary and the legislature requires the physical removal of the Law Lords from Parliament; fails to demonstrate how the proposed Supreme Court would exercise its functions with any greater degree of impartiality, independence and integrity than the Appellate Committee of the House of Lords; will deny Parliament the experience and expertise that the Law Lords bring to debates and legislation … and offers no convincing justification for replacing a system that works well."

Emboldened by an intervention from Edward Garnier, who hoped that his party "will ensure that it sticks up for what is good in this country and not allow the Labour Party to wash all over us the slack intellectual guff that it seems to be seduced by", Dominic Grieve declared that he "couldn't give a fig about the separation of powers" which had been invoked in support of the case for a supreme court. It was, he said, an 18th century concept that had been put together by a French philosopher who came over to this country and misunderstood the way in which the system worked. What mattered was the independence of the judiciary, a different concept altogether. A far more prolix (and somewhat meandering) contribution from his side of the House came from the former Secretary of State for the Environment in John Major's government, John Selwyn Gummer. His thesis, however, was simple. Since on the government's own admission, and as had been repeatedly emphasised when the debate was opened, the present system worked perfectly well without any complaint from the public, and the Law Lords were held in high esteem, it made far more political sense for the money which the government proposed to spend on the Supreme Court (£30 million plus) to be spent on more important matters such as climate change.

For the Liberal Democrats, their Constitutional Affairs spokesman, David Heath, welcomed the prospect of the Supreme Court. It would put an end, he said, to piling fiction upon fiction. The Appellate Committee of the House of Lords was an absurd and confusing name to give to our highest court; and as for the Law Lords, Lords of Appeal in Ordinary were "exactly what they [were] not, and nobody should suggest that they are." He thought that it would be helpful to the general public to understand that we have a supreme court that is a separate entity fulfilling a particular function. It was hardly a revolutionary proposal.

In the event the motion to reject a second reading of the bill was defeated by a predictably large majority, and the Commons then moved into its "Committee" stage. Dominic Grieve proceeded to table a couple of further amendments on the assumption that a supreme court would indeed come to pass. One required that the new Supreme Court should be located within the Palace of Westminster: an echo of the "Kingsland-Howe" amendment which had been defeated in the House of Lords; and the other that the Law Lords should be allowed to retain their titles: an echo of Lord Lloyd's unsuccessful amendment.

In support of those amendments, Dominic Grieve argued that only a minimal change was necessary. The Law Lords were insistent that they should continue to operate in an informal, committee room or seminar kind of setting; they had expressed their distaste for the Middlesex Guildhall – the only site "on offer"; there was no reason why an entirely separate supreme court could not be housed within the Palace of Westminster: after all, the United States Supreme Court was housed for many years inside the Congress Building; and the replicating of the informal setting of the Appellate Committee could be achieved at a minimal cost. Critically, the sunrise clause in the bill provided that the future home of the Supreme Court would first require the Law Lords' approval: he could not envisage the Guildhall as accommodating the kind of "habitat" which the Law Lords clearly had mind. Furthermore, what if English Heritage maintained its objection to the proposal? It was necessary to get planning permission, and the Guildhall was a Grade 2 listed building. He reminded the House that the facilities currently provided for the members of the Appellate Committee cost "the princely sum of £168,000"; this sum had to be compared with the enormous cost which would be incurred in refurbishing the Guildhall, and the knock-on cost which would be incurred in relocating and re-housing the seven criminal courts currently accommodated within the Guildhall. As to the Law Lords retaining their full membership of the

House of Lords on becoming Justices of the Supreme Court, their contribution to debates on law-related matters and to the work of legislative committees was considerable: they did not encroach on areas of potential embarrassment because of their scrupulous observance of well-established conventions. This Government, he observed, did not really believe in the value of conventions.

Ross Cranston, the former Labour Solicitor-General and a stalwart of the Constitutional Affairs Select Committee, explained that the notion behind having a supreme court was the rule of law and the independence of the judiciary: not, as Dominic Grieve seemed to think, separation of the powers. Just being seen as a *separate* court was not sufficient. What was important was that the court should be seen to function in a location *different* from the legislature. He didn't see any reason why a wholesale refurbishment of the Middlesex Guildhall could not accommodate courtrooms of the more informal style envisaged by the Law Lords. Simon Hughes, on behalf of the Liberal Democrats, agreed.

The amendments were in due course heavily defeated. Although the bill was concerned with issues which, as had always been anticipated, had raised a rather low level of interest among rank and file Labour MPs, and the debate had throughout been poorly attended on the government side, when it came to a vote, the division lobby filled rapidly. The bill returned to the House of Lords, and then finally received the Royal Assent on the 24th March 2005. The parliamentary process had taken just over one year to complete. The controversy around the issue of the Supreme Court was never going to be one capable of a quick resolution: a debate about the need for greater transparency, clarity and accessibility inevitably became very much a debate about political priorities, and had become interwoven with the wrangling over the survival of the office of Lord Chancellor, and whether a new-look Lord Chancellor needed to have legal qualifications and could sit in either the House of Lords or the House of Commons. To cap it all, the inauspicious circumstances surrounding the announcement of the policy which gave birth to the bill did not help. Probably, the case argued by the pragmatists would have been considerably stronger had they been able to point to building projects and improvements in the justice system on which the £32.5 million, plus "knock-on", capital costs, could have been spent instead. However, the government had made it clear that no projects or improvements would be sacrificed as result of allocating the proposed funding to the creation of the Supreme Court: this was one of the reasons which converted the Lord Chief Justice to the cause.

However, it was by no means going to be plain sailing from now on. Dominic Grieve had been right to remind everyone of the pivotal role of the sunrise clause. This had now become section 148 of the Constitutional Reform Act. This stated that those provisions which were relevant to the Supreme Court would only come into force if "the Lord Chancellor [was] satisfied that the Supreme Court [would be] provided with accommodation in accordance with written plans that he had approved"; and that such approval *had only been given after consultation "with the Lords of Appeal in Ordinary holding office at the time of [such] approval."* (Emphasis added) Then there were the further hurdles of obtaining listed building consent and planning permission, and the stance of English

Heritage. Furthermore, the well-known campaign group largely comprising architectural historians, Save Britain's Heritage, was uncompromisingly hostile to the project. All that said, one can assume that future historians will have few doubts about two propositions. First, legislating for a supreme court was something which would never have been contemplated by a Conservative government. Second, such legislation would in fact never have been contemplated by the Labour government of the day but for the little local difficulties concerning both the Lord Chancellor and the Lord Chancellor's Department.

# PART THREE
# The Court Emerges

## PLANS, DESIGNS AND MICRO-MANAGEMENT

The reader will recall the rather damning terms, expressed in a memorandum submitted to the Select Committee in April of the previous year on behalf of the Law Lords, in which Lord Bingham judged the suitability of the Middlesex Guildhall as the site for the prospective supreme court. An entry in Lord Hope's latest volume of diaries records what he describes as an "official visit" paid by all the Law Lords in the month following the submission of that memorandum. Apparently they were all overcome by the "gloomy and claustrophobic" atmosphere. He records that "attempts to suggest to us that a few cosmetic changes would do, were met with derision and disbelief. Tom's [Lord Bingham's] disgust was plain to see." However, Lady Hale recalls the visit a little differently. She has told the writer that in her own case she thought the site "was superb"; the exterior architecture (despite a century of grime) "impressive" and that there was "a wealth of exuberant interior decoration." Her impression was that her colleagues seemed to have difficulty in simply visualising how the interior could be both transformed and enhanced. In the event, the Department of Constitutional Affairs resolutely refused to be deflected by any expression of hostility on the part of the Law Lords and, as we have seen, by December 2004 the government had finally decided to go ahead with the Middlesex Guildhall as the chosen site.

Following the appointment of a leading firm of conservation architects (Fielden & Mawson) and Norman (Lord) Foster as consultant architect, detailed plans began to evolve. Presentations were made from time to time to groups of distinctly sceptical Law Lords, many of whom became increasingly less sceptical as time went on. So far as English Heritage was concerned, its view was that the existing courtroom interiors in the Guildhall were "unsurpassed by any other in the country built between the latter half of the nineteenth century and 1914 for their decorative richness and the completeness of their fittings." The ceilings were "splendid". (Of the seven Crown Courts accommodated within the building, the converted, rather grand former Council Chamber on the ground floor, was the *piece de resistance*.) Since the approval of English Heritage was crucial to the obtaining of listed building consent, the architects had the daunting task of come up with something which satisfied both the Law Lords *and* English Heritage.[30] They also had to liaise closely with the planning officers of Westminster City Council.

A serious problem arose at an early stage. The original plan was to locate the larger of the two courtrooms intended for Supreme Court hearings[31] in

---

[30]   How this was ultimately achieved is described in some detail in the lavishly illustrated coffee table  book *The Supreme Court of the United Kingdom: History. Art. Architecture* (Merrill, 2010) One of the conditions attached to the planning permission was that a commemorative book should be published, recording pictorially the features and condition of the Guildhall's interior prior to and after the building work had been carried out.

[31]   A third courtroom would be used for hearings of the Judicial Committee of the Privy Council, which at the time was accommodated in a building in Downing Street.

what was the former council chamber (and then the largest of the seven Crown Courts) situated in a central position on the ground floor. However, one of the Law Lords' requirements, which they regarded as "non-negotiable", was that the seating for the judges and counsel should be on the same level: (thus replicating the "committee" ambience.) This could not have been achieved in the use of the area enclosed by the former council chamber. Furthermore, having the courtroom located on the ground floor was thought to give rise to a significant security risk. Eventually Lord Foster's solution was to use this space at the very heart of the building for creating an impressive library, and locating both Supreme Court courtrooms on the upper floors. Agreement was reached with both English Heritage and the planning authorities as to the extent which "fixtures and fittings" and, crucially, furniture, could be removed. Planning and listed building consent were finally given in November 2005, subject inevitably to a number of conditions. One of them was that the conversion and refurbishment should contain high quality artwork. This explains why the renowned artist, Sir Peter Blake, was commissioned to design the courtroom carpets.

There was a twist in the tale. Whilst English Heritage proved to be accommodating, the campaign group, Save Britain's Heritage, expressed outrage at the granting of planning permission and brought judicial review proceedings to challenge the decision. Essentially, objection was taken to the approach which had been adopted by the planning officer in making his recommendation to the Council's Planning Committee: namely, to recognise the unique suitability of the site for the country's highest court, and to accept that the proposed scheme for adapting the building, though fairly drastic, significantly mitigated the impact which the redevelopment would have. It was argued that the planning officer got his priorities wrong. Before considering the suitability of the site in terms of location, he should have first asked the question whether the impact of the proposed works was such as to damage the features which were material to the listing of the building to the extent that permission should not be granted. Mr. Justice Collins rejected this argument. He pointed out that it "was clear there [would be] a major and damaging impact on the listed building …. It was therefore accepted that unless this was clearly the right place for the new court, the application [for planning and listed building consent] would be bound to fail. Thus it was necessary at the outset for the committee to be satisfied that this was indeed the right site." It was not until this hurdle had finally been overcome, that the building work really got under way.

Meanwhile, a sub-committee representing the interests of the Law lords had been set up to liaise with both the architects and the Department for Constitutional affairs. (The latter would later metamorphose into the Ministry of Justice in May 2007.) This sub-committee comprised Lords Hope and Mance, and Lady Hale. Each was given a special remit: Lady Hale had a particular responsibility for interior design; Lord Mance, for security; and Lord Hope for administration. (Later, Lady Hale would preside over an advisory Art panel.) A certain amount of micro-management now took over. Another requirement which the Law Lords regarded as "non-negotiable" was that the judges' seating should be curved or "horseshoe" shaped: (again, recreating the "committee" ambience.) Lady Hale ensured that this was followed through. There was a difference of opinion, however, as to the shape of counsels' seating and whether there should be a central podium arrangement such as in Committee Rooms 1 and 2 in the House of Lords. The majority view (favoured by both Lord Hope and Lady Hale) prevailed: counsels' seating arrangements would mirror those of the justices: the seating would be curved, and have individual lecterns rather than one central podium.

Over time a number of rather different issues had to be resolved by the Law Lords before the new Supreme Court was open for business. Famously, the Law Lords never wore gowns when sitting as members of the Appellate Committee. Should they do so now once they were sitting as Justices of the Supreme Court? All but one were opposed to wearing gowns except for ceremonial occasions: it was therefore agreed that gowns would not be worn. (Later, but only after the court had begun to function) it was agreed that counsel could dispense with wigs and gowns.) Again, in the Appellate Committee the custom was for the Law Lords to be seated before counsel could enter and take their places. Jenny Rowe, the Supreme Court's first Chief Executive (appointed in January 2008) recalls with amusement an arcane discussion whether this sequence should be adopted in the case of the brave new world of the Supreme Court. Very sensibly –one may think, – it was decided unanimously that the normal sequence should be followed: counsel should be in their seats *before* the justices made their entry into the courtroom. Then there was the question of how the judgment of the Supreme Court should be delivered. Should it be simply published and circulated, as was the case in some jurisdictions; or should the result of the appeal be announced in open court? It was decided that the latter should be the case, but without the necessity of the parties' lawyers having to be present.

The custom of the presiding justice providing a brief explanation of the issues and of the decision was introduced once the court was up and running, as was the case with the introduction of explanatory "press summaries" prepared for the benefit of the media. The contrast with the archaic ritual performed by the Law Lords when delivering judgment in the chamber of the House could not have been greater. As for the rules of procedure and practice directions, they were later devised and developed in close consultation with members of the Court of Appeal, High Court judges and representatives from the Bar and the Law Society.

## THE SUPREME COURT
## ESTABLISHES ITSELF

The building work and refurbishment took exactly one year longer than had been originally planned, but the result was impressive: a skilful blending of the "old" with the new, thus confounding the gloomy expectations of many. It will be recalled that Lord Neill for instance, in the "amendment" debate, said that "the certainties were that there would be an overrun on cash and an overrun on time", and that "the probability was that the building would be ugly." He was proved correct in respect of his former, but very much wide of the mark in respect of the latter.

The Supreme Court for the United Kingdom opened for business at the beginning of October 2009, and was officially opened by the Queen on the 16th October. Its arch apostle, Lord Bingham, had already retired the previous year. Only two of the original eleven justices still remain in post: Lady Hale, who is now President of the Court, and Lord Kerr. All eleven were life peers at the time of their appointment to the Supreme Court, and one vacancy had still to be filled. When eventually it was filled six months later, it brought to light an unresolved problem. In the knowledge that when the vacancy came to be filled, the strong probability was that new justice would be appointed from the ranks of the Court of Appeal, Jenny Rowe, the Chief Executive, raised more than once the question with both the Ministry of Justice and the President of the Court, Lord Phillips: how should the newly appointed justice be referred to in court by his or her fellow justices and by counsel? Presumably he or she could not be referred to as Lord or Lady X, since he or she was not, like everyone else, a life peer? No answer was forthcoming. The failure to grasp this particular nettle was cruelly exposed when the next appointee did indeed come from the Court of Appeal. When Lord Justice Dyson was appointed to fill the vacancy in April 2010, he had to endure the irritation and embarrassment for several months of being referred to as "Sir John Dyson", whereas all his male colleagues were referred as "Lord ------". Eventually the problem was solved by the expedient of the Queen signing a royal warrant conferring the courtesy title of "Lord" or "Lady" automatically on all appointees to the Supreme Court.[32]

But apart from this solitary lapse, the micro-management and attention to detail which preceded the opening of the court in October 2009 proved to

[32] This was not Jenny Rowe's (nor for that matter, Lady Hale's) preferred solution, as it appeared to them to be gender discriminatory in its effect: whereas wives of male justices would be known as "Lady X", the husbands of female justices would have no such recognition. Their preferred solution was to apply literally the wording of the legislation: "The judges other than the President and the Deputy President are to be styled 'Justices of the Supreme Court.'" In other words, they should have been referred in court simply as "Justice X."

be highly successful. In terms of public awareness and accessibility, the impact of the new court was immediate and obvious. Live streaming of all hearings (introduced a little later), a dedicated website, closed circuit TV, an information centre and a café all combined to fulfil one of the avowed aims of the campaigners and advocates for change. Coach parties of schoolchildren and students have been a regular feature: albeit the attention span is inevitably limited, and the average time spent inside one or other of the two courtrooms therefore has been twenty- five to thirty minutes. Years later, TV and livestreaming would come into its own in the Article 50 (Brexit) case: there can be little doubt that the extent of the exposure of the entire proceedings to the public gaze minimised the risk of another "Enemies of the People" reaction from sections of the media, as of course did the explanatory press summary. And contrary to the prediction voiced repeatedly in the House of Lords debates, there has been no evidence of confusion in the minds of the public as to the court's function and powers. Specifically, there has been no evidence that the general public believes its powers and functions are comparable to those exercised by the Supreme Court of the United States.

But all that said, the important question is whether the change from the Appellate Committee of the House of Lords to the Supreme Court has made any difference in terms of the *substantive* decision-making; and in particular whether the performance of the court over the first ten years of its existence, in terms of both approach and the nature of its actual decisions, has confirmed the fears expressed not only by politicians but by former Law Lords that the court would inevitably over the course of time assume a role, and exercise powers, reminiscent of the Supreme Court of the United States. Before considering those questions, however, it is worth mentioning the changes which have been introduced in the way the court has gone about its work, some of which have been quite striking.

The use of enlarged panels of seven or more justices is an obvious example. During the last ten years of the Appellate Committee's existence, enlarged panels were deployed on only thirteen occasions. In the case of the Supreme Court, in the first four years of its operation, under the Presidency of Lord Phillips, enlarged appeals featured frequently, including panels of nine; and not solely in cases involving public law and human rights issues, as had been predicted. The issue in one of the very first appeals to be heard by the court back in October 2009 and which was heard by a panel of nine, was whether a voluntarily aided, and over-subscribed, Jewish comprehensive school was entitled to refuse admission to a child whose mother was not recognised as Jewish by the Office of the Chief Rabbi. (A majority decision of the Appellate Committee some twenty years previously had concluded that motive was irrelevant in determining whether there had been discrimination on the ground of sex or race.) Less than a year later a nine member panel was twice convened: on one occasion to hear an appeal which concerned the question of the enforceability of pre-nuptial agreements; and on another, to hear an appeal concerning a soldier who suffered heatstroke whilst on operational duties in Iraq, which raised the issue of whether the European Convention on Human Rights had in certain circumstances extra-territorial effect. Under the Presidency of Lord Phillips' successor, Lord Neuberger, less use was made of enlarged panels: "We calmed down a little", Lady Hale told the writer. A notable exception was of course the use of an eleven member panel in the Article 50 case: something that would not have been readily contemplated in the days of the old Appellate Committee. Another exception was when a nine member panel sat in an appeal which raised the question of the legality or otherwise of assisted suicide, and specifically the incompatibility or otherwise of the Suicide Act with the European Convention on Human Rights.

Whether there have been other significant changes in the way the court has gone about its work in the context of what may be described as the "dynamics" of its decision-making is more questionable. There has been much discussion about whether there has been less disagreement and more signs of "collegiality" than was the case with the old Appellate Committee. During the first four years of the court's existence (under the Presidency of Lord Phillips) the frequency of dissenting judgments ran at 26% of the court's decisions. This was in fact broadly the same frequency of dissent experienced in the days of the Appellate Committee, and was hardly surprising. Lord Phillips, who had been the Senior Law Lord in the last year of the Appellate Committee, had what a former Justice of the Supreme Court has described as a *laissez faire* attitude: he had no particular interest in imposing a "single judgment" policy, and normally held only one post-hearing conference. In one instance, involving a seven member panel, although the appeal succeeded by a majority of six to one, there were five separate judgments, and the majority were evenly split as to the reason for their decision, each of the two factions rejecting the reason relied on by the other.

Lord Neuberger, on succeeding Lord Phillips as President, had a rather different approach. In much publicized comments following his appointment he said that one of his aims was to reduce the level of dissent and thereby enhance the authority of the court. Initially he succeeded. Over a period of eight months there was an unbroken succession of single judgment decisions, prompting one eminent academic lawyer, Professor Alan Paterson of Strathclyde University, who has over several years made a special study of the habits of the Law Lords and, latterly, the Supreme Court Justices, to worry whether we had witnessed the end of "judicial individualism".[33] He attributed this trend in part to a greater amount of teamwork and collegiality,[34] involving a more collaborative approach. However, the trend did not continue throughout Lord Neuberger's presidency: in the assisted suicide case, for example, each of the nine members of the panel delivered a separate judgment; and the frequency of dissent reverted to the same level as under the presidency of Lord Phillips. And as occasionally happened in the days of the Appellate Committee, one still comes across the odd case where the diversity of view expressed in multiple judgments can from the practising lawyer's point of view create a degree of uncertainty and lack of clarity. For instance, in a recent decision involving the alleged infringement of a patent for a pharmaceutical drug, separate judgements were delivered by all five members of the panel. On one issue the court was unanimous; on another there

[33] His recourse to statistical breakdowns and graphs is rather similar to how social anthropologists apply themselves to the study of social, racial and national groupings.
[34] Some former Law Lords who have also sat in the Supreme Court, when questioned by the writer on the subject, have responded with polite scepticism to this explanation. In their view there was no discernible difference in terms of collegiality between the Appellate Committee and the Supreme Court: they were, in their view, equally "collegial" places in which to work, although the latter undoubtedly had the better amenities to achieve such a result – e.g. conference room, dining room.

was a majority of three to two; and on the third issue, whilst there was unanimity in the result, each of the justices gave a different and conflicting reason. This kind of situation would not infrequently occur in the days of the Appellate Committee. However, occasional disagreement is not inconsistent with a more collaborative approach when this is possible. Recently, the Deputy President of the court, Lord Reed, has publicly made it clear that a single judgment was the preferred objective in most cases, and that where this has proved to be case it has usually reflected a collaborative effort on the part of all members of the panel, often involving more than one meeting.[35] And is not without significance that a recent advertisement inviting applications to fill prospective vacancies on the Supreme Court, specifies "an ability to contribute to the collegiate decision-making of the Court" as one of the necessary attributes.

What has attracted little comment, however, is the change that has clearly occurred in the manner that disagreement *has come to be expressed* in judgments delivered by the Supreme Court. In the era of the Appellate Committee, a Law Lord would rarely refer in his judgment to the judgments of his colleagues, let alone their arguments, even where there had been disagreement. This was largely the result of the format of those judgments: they were technically *speeches*, delivered in order of seniority. Released from these quaint constraints, In the new era horns are properly locked: the difference of view is met head on with specific reference to passages in fellow Justices' judgments. In one instance Lord Neuberger went to the length of devoting an entire section of his

---

[35] The Bentham Association Lecture 2019, UCL.

judgment, headed "The different views expressed in other judgments", to the respective judgments of three dissenting, or partially dissenting, Justices. In an earlier case Lord Wilson, who had only recently been appointed to the Supreme Court, began his judgment with the words: "In my view the approach of Lord Phillips, Baroness Hale and Lord Kerr to the meaning of the word "knowledge" in the ... Limitation Act 1980 is misconceived, and would throw the practical application of [the relevant provisions] into disarray." Arguably such explicit expressions of disagreement can be viewed as a positive development in terms of achieving greater transparency and clarity, but they would have been unthinkable under the old regime.

## NO "RUSH OF BLOOD TO THE HEAD"

Mindful of some of the predictions which enlivened the debates in Parliament, the question has to be asked: has the arrival of the Supreme Court made any difference either in regard to the kind of cases which are nowadays decided at the highest level, or in regard to *how* those cases are decided? Or put another way, has the fear that the Supreme Court would venture into areas where the Appellate Committee of the House of Lords would have been reluctant to tread, and/or in any way challenge or encroach upon the sovereignty of Parliament, proved to be unfounded? In other words, have there been any tell-tale signs of – to use Lord Bingham's words when giving evidence to the Lords Select Committee – any "rush of the blood to the head"? Ten years is certainly a long enough time span to allow one to answer those questions with some confidence.

It needs to be emphasised that the Supreme Court is required to apply precisely the same criteria for granting permission to appeal as had formerly been applied by the Appellate Committee, and indeed has consistently done so. In short, there has to be an important (and usually difficult) point of law involved, which needs to be resolved in the public interest. It is first worth taking a brief look at the range of cases which the Appellate Committee had decided during its one hundred and thirty three year history.

That range is in fact quite remarkable. Many cases involved the seemingly banal circumstances of everyday life, of which perhaps the most famous instance was the "snail in the ginger beer bottle" case of *Donoghue v Stevenson*, which first established that the manufacturer of a product could be liable in negligence to the ultimate consumer. That case of course was decided in the early 1930s, but there was no shortage of such cases in more recent times. A striking instance was when by a majority of three to two it was decided that a solicitor could owe a duty of care to prospective beneficiaries under a will which he had been instructed to draw up, where the beguilingly simple facts were that following a reconciliation in the wake of a family row, a father had instructed the solicitor to change his will to provide legacies for his two daughters, but died before the solicitor had got around to complying with the father's instructions, the delay having been found to be inexcusable. Another such instance was when the Appellate Committee had to decide whether a local council which operated a swimming pool at its leisure centre, was guilty of unlawful sex discrimination when it refused free use of the swimming pool to a sixty one year old gentleman, but allowed free access to the pool to his wife, who was of the same age. That he was not yet in receipt of a state pension, whereas his wife was, was not regarded by a majority of the Appellate Committee as a lawful justification for the difference in treatment. Then on the other hand there were many memorable cases raising important issues in terms of both policy and principle involving the government of the day: for example, cases concerning detention without trial such as the celebrated wartime case of *Liversidge v Anderson* (detention of a naturalised civilian under the Emergency Regulations), and of course more recently the Belmarsh case, which concerned detention under the anti-terror legislation. There were many other instances such as the *Spycatcher* case, concerning the unauthorised publication of the memoirs of a former employee of MI5; the case brought by a Mrs. Gillick concerning the legality of contraceptive advice for under sixteen girls which had been issued by the Department of Health and Social Security; and the cases revolving around the issue whether damages were recoverable in respect of an unwanted child in negligence claims brought against hospital trusts.

The truth is that the cases which have characterised the workload of the Supreme Court have been just as wide-ranging. Although in the very early years of its existence the aftermath of the Iraq war, a plethora of immigration cases, and perennial problems created by the anti-terror legislation all combined to produce a crop of appeals concerning human rights issues, with the Home Office invariably in the firing line, a look at the appeals which the Supreme Court has heard during the last two years should dispel any lingering doubt that its function has assumed some sort of constitutional role. The variety and range of cases have certainly been comparable to that heard by the Appellate Committee of the House of Lords. The following cross-section of cases will give the reader a flavour.

The court was required to decide whether a contact for the letting of office premises, which expressly provides that none of its terms could be subsequently varied by any *oral* agreement entered into by the parties, could nevertheless be varied by an oral agreement. In other words, the issue was whether the parties could fetter their own otherwise autonomous right to contract as they chose: a point that has long troubled lawyers and given rise to conflicting views. (A great American judge, Justice Cardozo, once famously opined that "[t]hose who make a contract, may unmake it …. Whenever two men contract, no limitation self-imposed can destroy their power to contract again …") In this particular case the credit controller of the landlord company had orally agreed a reduction in the rent specified in the tenancy agreement with a director of the tenant company. The Supreme Court decided that the oral agreement was unenforceable, and the original terms of the letting agreement were the operative ones.

The court had shortly afterwards occasion to grapple with another quasi-philosophical question: can one bring a claim for damages against a person whose identity and address was unknown? The driver of a car had been injured as result of a collision caused by the unidentified driver of another vehicle. That vehicle had been insured under a policy issued to a person who the insurer subsequently believed to be fictitious. The injured driver claimed damages against "the person unknown driving vehicle registration number … who collided with vehicle registration number … on 26 May 2013"; and sought a declaration that the insurer would be liable to meet any judgment obtained against that person. The insurer resisted the claim. The Court of Appeal had decided by a majority that the injured driver was entitled to pursue her claim but the Supreme Court (unanimously) decided otherwise. Cars and car insurers coincidentally formed the backcloth to another appeal. A car caught fire whilst being repaired by its owner, causing damage to adjoining property. The car was insured to cover third party damage and injury in respect of its use, but was it in "use" at the relevant time? The Supreme Court decided it was not.

Then there was the gay wedding cake case involving a bakery in Northern Ireland. A baker refused a commission to bake an inscribed wedding cake for a gay couple on religious grounds: did this constitute unlawful discrimination on the ground of sexual orientation? The Supreme Court decided that it did not. In sharp contrast, the court heard a case involving a dispute concerning two of the most demonised figures in everyday commercial life: a property developer and an estate agent. The issue was whether an oral agreement reached on the telephone between the property developer and the estate agent was enforceable where, following the sale of the property in question, the precise circumstances in which the commission became payable had not been spelt out. The court decided it was.

Finally, to round off this *tour d' horizon* of cases heard by the Supreme Court over the last two years, there was a case of a kind which could have been decided by the Appellate Committee at any time during the latter years of its existence, and which would have divided opinion in the same manner. The point at issue had indeed, at least to lawyers, something of a timeless charm about it. In the course of deciding whether an employee of an NHS hospital trust had completed twenty years of service so as to entitle her to an early retirement pension, the court had to consider whether a written notice of twelve weeks to terminate her employment on the ground of redundancy, sent by letter to her home whilst she was still on holiday, took effect when the letter would have been delivered in the ordinary course of post, or when the letter actually first came to her to attention. If the latter, she had indeed completed twenty years of employment. In order to resolve that issue, the Supreme Court found it necessary to consider some picaresque landlord and tenant cases of the 18th and 19th century, all concerned with the service of a notice to quit. The five justices who heard the appeal were divided in their interpretation as to what those cases actually decided, and were therefore equally divided as to whether the appeal by the NHS employee should succeed. Whilst the majority decided that it should, the two justices in the minority took the view that those old cases conclusively demonstrated that written notice of termination of a "relational" contract is properly given once it is either hand-delivered or posted to the recipient's home: *not* when the notice comes to his or her personal attention: a temporary absence, or a mishap such as the family dog eating the letter, were, in their view, "a risk which the law allocates to the recipient." One can envisage many a Law Lord in the old Appellate Committee reasoning on these lines.

But what if one focuses on the court's treatment of those cases which by contrast involve government departments, public policy, and the like: does one then spot any change since the days of the Appellate Committee in any of those ways that were feared? This question has in a way acquired a certain topicality as a result of the recent Reith Lectures given by the former Supreme Court Justice, Lord Sumption. In those lectures he developed a theme which he first touched upon in a public lecture delivered shortly before he was appointed to the Supreme Court: namely, that in deciding cases concerning decisions and actions by government departments and other public authorities, the courts (at different levels) were slipping into the habit of reviewing the actual policy and merits of the legislation under which the decisions or actions were taken. In short, judges were applying what were essentially their own value judgments: they were not applying or invoking principles of law. In other words, the law was in danger of intruding into areas into which it has no business to intrude.

A look at a representative cross-section of those public law-related cases decided over the last ten years, would suggest that the answer to the question is also an emphatic No. One should perhaps start with the highest profile case of them all: the Article 50 case. The issue, it will be recalled, was whether the government was entitled to give notice of its intention to withdraw from the European Union under Article 50 of the Treaty of Lisbon in the exercise of its powers under the royal prerogative, without requiring the authority of Parliament. The Supreme Court, by a majority of eight to three, decided it could not. It did so on the ground that the European Communities Act 1972 (which ratified the Treaty of Rome as part of our domestic law) authorised a process by which EU law became a source of UK law which took precedence over all other sources of law, and long as that Act remained in force, it could only be repealed by another Act of Parliament. One can of course be critical of the reasoning, as indeed were the three dissentients, but no one suggested that the majority decision itself was one which the court was not entitled to make. Indeed, even those sections of the media which had been outspokenly critical of the judgment of the Divisional Court against which the government had appealed, made any such suggestion. In fact a not dissimilar issue (though of course not so momentous) had confronted the Appellate Committee some thirty years previously, when it was required to decide whether certain provisions of the Merchant Shipping Act 1988 should be declared to be unlawful because, so it was claimed, they were in direct conflict with provisions of the Treaty of Rome and certain EEC rules. The Law Lords declined to make such declaration.

In a number of cases, particularly those involving issues of human rights and fair dealing, the approach of the court has to a large extent this has been dominated by the concept of "proportionality": inevitably so, ever since the incorporation of the European Convention on Human Rights into our domestic law by virtue of the Human Rights Act 1998, and the impact of judgments of the European Court of Human Rights. Indeed, the concept had not infrequently been applied in the days of the Appellate Committee. Two very different cases illustrate the way the Supreme Court has applied the concept, one in the "early" years under the presidency of Lord Phillips, and the other under the presidency of Lord Neuberger.

The first case concerned one of the government's measures to combat what was perceived to be the problem of forced marriages. Regulations were introduced which precluded persons to enter or remain in the United Kingdom as a spouse of someone lawfully resident and settled in the United Kingdom if either party to the marriage was under the age of twenty- one.

They superseded regulations which specified eighteen as the relevant age. The decision to increase the age bar apparently reflected recommendations contained in an unpublished report by the House of Commons Home Affairs Select Committee, and conclusions reached by the Home Secretary based on internal reports and research. An appeal brought by a young married couple – she, a 17 year old British girl, he, an 18 year old Chilean who had entered the UK on a student visa and had been refused permission to remain, raised the question whether the regulation breached Article 8 (1) of the European Convention of Human Rights: the right to respect for private and family life. The majority decided that it did. They thought it amounted to a "colossal interference" with the exercise of such right, and one which could not be justified. Both the research and the report relied on by the Home Office, they thought, were deeply flawed, and the raising of the age bar from eighteen to twenty-one was simply not a "proportionate response" to the problem of forced marriages. In the words of the Justice who delivered the leading judgment, increasing the age bar amounted to "using a sledgehammer to crack a nut." There was, however, a vigorous dissenting judgment from Lord Brown, who took the view that it was quite wrong for the majority to delve into the merits of the thinking behind the decision to increase the age bar, and very much anticipating the line of thought which was subsequently to be developed in lectures by Lord Sumption, he warned of "dire consequences if the trend towards active intervention by the courts continued."

The second case concerned an intervention by the Treasury. Under provisions of the counter-terrorism legislation the Treasury was empowered to take steps to restrict the access of banks to the UK financial market if there was a risk such access would lead to nuclear proliferation. The Treasury sought to impose such restriction on a UK subsidiary of an Iranian bank suspected of having links with Iran's nuclear and ballistics programme. The bank challenged the legality of the Treasury's action, seeking to have the restriction lifted. It succeeded. The Supreme Court (comprising a panel of nine) decided by a substantial majority that the restriction imposed on this particular bank was not a "proportionate response" to the risk that the bank's activity in the financial market could contribute to nuclear proliferation. There appeared to be no justification for singling out this bank in particular, when there were many others with suspected links to the Iranian nuclear programme. They thought the position was analogous to that considered by the House of Lords in the Belmarsh case, where it was held that the detention of foreign nationals, whose presence in the UK was considered by the Home Secretary to be a risk to national security but could not be deported, was a disproportionate response to the terrorist threat which had provoked it.

The majority decisions in both these cases might have been described by those of a "Sir Humphrey" cast of mind as "bold", but in fact only the decision in the foreign spouses case could really be said to be in any way eyebrow-raising: delving with a critical eye into the thinking and research which accounted for the passing of a regulation was not an exercise on which judges were usually inclined to embark when deciding whether that regulation was enforceable as a matter of law. (Had of course the age bar been enshrined in an Act of Parliament and not in a statutory instrument (as in this case), the court would only have had the power to make a "declaration of incompatibility". This is exactly what it did in respect of the Civil Partnership Act, judged to be discriminatory against heterosexual couples.)

In fact the Supreme Court has more often than not proceeded with caution in cases where social policy issues are involved. For example, in the assisted suicide case, the majority decided that in principle the court was entitled to declare provisions of the Suicide Act incompatible with the European Convention on Human Rights, but that they were not inclined to so without first giving Parliament a further opportunity to consider the matter. Their reluctance in truth reflected precisely the same considerations which prompted the minority to conclude that the court was *not* entitled to make a declaration of incompatibility: namely, to do so would involve taking a view on sensitive issues which Parliament was inherently better qualified than the courts to assess. Another instance was when the court was required to consider whether legal advice privilege, which confers immunity from disclosure of legal advice to third parties and has been part of our common law for nearly two centuries, could extend beyond communications between lawyers and their clients, to legal advice given by members of other professions – such as chartered accountants. By a majority of five to two the court decided that legal advice privilege could not be so extended. In delivering the majority judgment, Lord Neuberger pointed out that the scope of the privilege was an area into which the court should be reluctant to tread. It raised sensitive policy issues which were pre-eminently a matter for Parliament, having been the subject of discussion by a Parliamentary select committee, and Parliament having legislated in certain areas on the basis that legal advice privilege was indeed confined to communications with lawyers.

To complete the picture of how the Supreme Court has handled cases with a public law dimension, mention must be made of two notable defeats suffered by the government – less spectacular perhaps than that suffered in the Article 50 case, but nonetheless quite striking in their different ways. One concerned the occasional and well publicized correspondence of Prince Charles with certain ministers on matters dear to his heart. Under the provisions of the Freedom of Information Act, the Attorney General was empowered to issue a certificate preventing disclosure of documents if he had reasonable grounds for doing so. In this instance the Upper Tribunal, reversing a decision of the Information Tribunal, had ruled that the Prince's correspondence could be disclosed. The Attorney General decided to intervene, and issued a certificate to prevent its disclosure. The Supreme Court decided that he was not entitled to do so, primarily on the ground that it is a basic principle that a decision of a court is binding as between the parties, and cannot be set aside by anyone, including – and least of all – by the executive.

The other defeat worthy of mention concerned the introduction of fees for bringing claims in the employment tribunals: previously access to the tribunals had been free of charge. The government brought in regulations which required payment of fees at two stages: first when the claim was brought, and secondly prior to the final hearing. The rationale relied on by the government for this radical change was that it was wrong in principle that taxpayers should have to fund a service which the majority of people don't use, and that therefore the imposing of fees would result in the transfer of part of the cost burden from the taxpayer to the user of the service. The legality of the scheme was challenged by a union, members of which were likely at some point to have recourse to employment tribunals. The challenge succeeded. The Supreme Court declared the fee charging scheme to be unlawful on the ground that it violated the fundamental common law principle of unimpeded access to justice, which was integral to the rule of law; and that the rationale behind its introduction relied on by the government was flawed. The fallacy in the government's thinking, so the Supreme Court held, was the assumption that access to the courts or tribunals was only of value to the individuals involved. Lord Reed, in delivering the lead judgment, pointed out that when Mrs. Donoghue (of *Donoghue v Stevenson* fame) brought her appeal in the House of Lords, the decision – one of the most important of the twentieth century – established the circumstances in which producers of consumer goods could be liable in respect of the safety of the consumer, and that it would be absurd to say that her appeal was of value *only to her and her lawyers*. Furthermore, the value to society in having unimpeded access to employment tribunals lay in the need for employees to know that they would be able to enforce their rights if they have to do so, and for employers to know that if they failed to meet their obligations, there was likely to be a remedy against them.

In neither of these cases can it be plausibly argued that the Supreme Court displayed a mindset which marked some sort of departure from that which characterised the Appellate Committee of the House of Lords. In both case cases the issue was resolved by invoking basic principles. The Appellate Committee was not itself averse to invoking basic principles, nor, for that matter, making moral value judgments: the *Spycatcher* and *Gillick* cases are classic illustrations of this. The invoking of moral principles, for example, determined the outcome in the cases concerned with the award of damages in respect of an unwanted (but otherwise healthy) child; and in fact much of the law of negligence concerned with the liability of public authorities has been shaped by social policy (in turn based on individual value judgments) developed over the years by the Law Lords. In other words, there has been no discernible change in approach where the court has been required to engage with novel situations. It is precisely because there has been a sense of continuity, that the replacement of the Appellate Committee by the Supreme Court has been accepted so quickly by the general public, the media and the legal profession. Bearing in mind the fierce Parliamentary battles and extravagant rhetoric which preceded its arrival on the legal scene, this inevitably prompts one to ask: apart from the small matter of the capital cost and the running costs involved, what on earth was all the fuss about!?

# A New Supreme Court for the United Kingdom

## The Constitution Unit Spring Lecture 2002
## by Lord Bingham of Cornhill
### 1 May 2002

I think it is generally true, in the lives of nations as of individual human beings, that many significant events, if not the product of pure chance, are certainly not the product of considered decision or deep design. Such is surely true of the supreme judicial power exercised by the House of Lords. It seems unlikely that any person or body of people consciously decided to devolve the ultimate judicial authority within the country formerly vested in a personal monarch on this chamber of the legislature. But by Tudor or Stuart times it had come to be recognised that this transfer had been effected.

By that time of course there existed a corps of professional judges who, at a lower level, exercised judicial power on behalf and in the name of the crown. It must always have been faintly anomalous to entrust a legislative body, largely made up of members with no judicial experience or legal knowledge, with the power to review the decisions of these judges. The usual justification for such an arrangement is that whatever the theoretical anomaly it works well in practice. But in this instance, at any rate by the eighteenth and nineteenth centuries, the arrangement did not work well at all. One may point to the year 1811 in which the House heard 23 appeals but had a backlog of 266 waiting to be heard. Even this however compared well with the Judicial Committee of the Privy Council which normally sat for judicial business only on 9 feast days but was said in 1828 to have 517 cases awaiting disposal. The Solicitor General was perhaps guilty of understatement when he said of the House of Lords in 1855 that "judicial business was conducted before the Supreme Court of Appeal in a manner which would disgrace the lowest court of justice in the kingdom".

A situation so dire could not endure indefinitely. But repeated attempts during the nineteenth century to merge the House of Lords and the Privy Council in their judicial capacities were thwarted, and there was—not surprisingly—a strong body of support for a proposal, which was enacted but never brought into force, that the appellate jurisdiction of the House of Lords in relation to England and Wales should be abolished. In the event, the right of appeal was preserved, largely because the loss of its appellate jurisdiction was seen at the time as damaging to the prestige of the House of Lords. But the jurisdiction survived only because its exercise was professionalised pursuant to the Appellate Jurisdiction Act 1876, as the Privy Council had been professionalised five years earlier.

In the years since 1876 the House of Lords in its judicial capacity has by no means escaped criticism. But I know of no final court in any major jurisdiction which has escaped criticism and that directed to the House of Lords has not, I think, by international standards, been particularly severe. Most would, I think, agree that the House has, not least in relatively recent times, included among its members judges of outstanding distinction, erudition and wisdom.

The suggestion, raised by influential and authoritative voices as recently as the 1960s, that there should be no appeal beyond the Court of Appeal is now rarely, if ever, heard. But the future of the Appellate Committee of the House of Lords and the Judicial Committee of the Privy Council have again, for the first time since the 1870s, become a topic of continuing debate, addressed by distinguished academic commentators, including Andrew le Sueur and Richard Cornes and others, discussed by professional bodies and commentators and seen by the Constitution Unit as part of the current national agenda of constitutional reform. Until recently the published literature on this subject has been, in quantity, relatively modest. Why has it now become topical? I think there are perhaps three main reasons.

The first is obvious. It is that the composition of the House of Lords itself has been significantly changed and further change is promised (or, as some would see it, threatened). Lord Wakeham's commission saw no reason why a reformed second chamber should not continue to exercise the judicial functions of the existing House of Lords, but it was not asked to advise whether it was appropriate that the House of Lords should continue to exercise judicial functions at all, and it is perhaps unlikely that the House of Lords will emerge from the current bout of reform in the shape that the commission recommended. Anyone not equipped with a crystal ball in good working order must necessarily be cautious in making any prediction about the ultimate shape of a reformed House. The process of change seems currently to have lost some of its momentum, and it may no doubt be that the interim solution adopted in 1999 will prove as durable as that adopted in 1911. If, however, it be assumed that the process of change will continue, it would seem to me on the whole likely that a reformed House will differ from the existing House in three respects at least: it will contain a substantial elected element, perhaps as much as a half or more, with, in addition, an appointed cross-bench membership; its overall size will be smaller; and the demands made on the time and attendance of members will be greater. If this prediction is even broadly correct, certain consequences follow. The power to recruit independent cross- bench members of the House will be curtailed. Such membership, an increasingly rare privilege, will be reserved for those who are judged to have most to contribute, by virtue of their knowledge or professional qualifications or previous experience, to the business of the House. Thus there will, on the assumption that an independent appointed cross-bench element continues, be places for some distinguished ex-service chiefs and doctors and diplomats and so on. But there will obviously be resistance to the recruitment of those (like the serving law lords) who, because of their professional inhibitions and the other demands upon them, cannot play a full part as members of the House. The smaller the House, the stronger the resistance to such non-playing members will inevitably be. It would furthermore seem likely that even if the overall size of the House is smaller, the demands on its accommodation and facilities will be greater: the space occupied by the law lords will then be viewed even more jealously than it is now.

The second reason why, as I think, the judicial role of the House of Lords has recently attracted unwonted attention is related to the Human Rights Act and its incorporation of the European Convention. The Convention jurisprudence has encouraged a stricter view to be taken not only of anything which does or may in fact undermine the independence or impartiality of a judicial tribunal but also of anything which might, on its face, appear to do so. In this country in recent years the separation of the judicial authorities on the one hand from the executive and legislative authorities on the other has been all but total. But the Convention is concerned with risks and appearances as well as actualities.

In *Findlay v United Kingdom* [1997] 24 EHRR 221 a soldier who had pleaded guilty at his court martial successfully challenged the court martial procedure on the ground that the same senior officer had convened the court martial, appointed its members (junior to him but within his chain of command), appointed the prosecuting and defending officer, had had power to dissolve the court martial and had had power to ratify the court martial's decision. The European Court said (paragraph 73):

> "In order to establish whether a tribunal can be considered as 'independent', regard must be had inter alia to the manner of appointment of its members and their term of office, the existence of guarantees against outside pressures and the question whether the body presents an appearance of independence.
>
> As to the question of 'impartiality', there are two aspects to this requirement. First, the tribunal must be subjectively free of personal prejudice or bias. Secondly, it must also be impartial from an objective viewpoint, that is, it must offer

sufficient guarantees to exclude any legitimate doubt in this respect".

It has more recently been held (*Morris v UK*, 26 February 2002, Application No 00038784 / 97) that there were insufficient safeguards to exclude the risk of outside pressure being brought to bear on the two relatively junior officers who had sat on a court martial, although there was nothing to suggest that any outside pressure of any kind had in fact been brought to bear on them. In *Starrs v Ruxton* 2000 JC 208 there was no reflection on the conduct, propriety or integrity (pages 213D, 234C) of the temporary sheriff whose role was successfully challenged, but Lord Reed (at page 250E) said:

"The effect given to the European Convention by the Scotland Act and the Human Rights Act in particular represents, to my mind, a very important shift in thinking about the constitution. It is fundamental to that shift that human rights are no longer dependent solely on convention, by which I mean values, customs and practices of the constitution which are not legally enforceable. Although the Convention protects rights which reflect democratic values and underpin democratic institutions, the Convention guarantees the protection of those rights through legal processes, rather than political processes. It is for that reason that Article 6 guarantees access to independent courts. It would be inconsistent with the whole approach of the Convention if the independence of those courts rested upon convention rather than law."

126

So, in *Millar v Dickson* 2002 UKPC 30 the challenge under article 6 succeeded even though the conduct of all the temporary sheriffs involved was accepted as having been impeccable and there was no reason to think that any of the accused had suffered any substantial injustice. It was again the duality of his role, as legislator and judge, which undid the Bailiff of Guernsey: *McGonnell v United Kingdom* (2000) 30 EHRR 289. It was held that the applicant had legitimate grounds for fearing that the Bailiff might have been influenced by his prior participation in the adoption of a planning policy: that doubt, however slight its justification, was sufficient to vitiate the impartiality of the court (page 308, paragraph 57.)

As with independence, so with impartiality. The public are increasingly sceptical of a judge's ability to lay his or her personal views and opinions to one side when sitting judicially. I myself consider that this scepticism is largely misplaced. But cases can occur, and have occurred, when a statement has been made out of court in terms so outspoken and uncompromising as to throw doubt on the judge's ability to be objective and impartial in court: see *Locabail (UK) Limited v Bayfield Properties Ltd* [2000] QB 451, 496; *Hoekstra v Her Majesty's Advocate* [2000] Scot HC 32. The result has been to fortify the tradition, already strong, of judicial reticence and to strengthen the steadily growing reluctance of the Law Lords to participate in the legislative business of the House. If however, a habit of reticence makes for good judges, it makes for poor legislators and debaters, and serves to weaken the justification for including the Law Lords among the members of the House.

The third reason why the supreme court question has attracted attention is perhaps more tenuous. It relates to the devolution settlement and the new role of the Privy Council as the arbiter of demarcation questions between the central government and the devolved institutions. Until relatively recent times, even to the minority who had heard of it at all, the Judicial Committee of the Privy Council had, I think, come to be seen as a body in its death throes. In some respects its jurisdiction was recognised to be plainly anomalous and overdue for transfer elsewhere, for example in hearing medical disciplinary appeals. Its overseas jurisdiction was seen to be steadily shrinking: New Zealand, the surviving jewel in its crown, had more than once announced its intention to abolish the right of appeal; a number of Caribbean jurisdictions had announced their intention to establish their own court of appeal locally; what remained could scarcely keep the Judicial Committee in business. But its new role in the devolution settlement plainly gives the Judicial Committee an enhanced role and much greater prominence in the United Kingdom context. Thus, for instance, the Advocate General for Scotland, the Lord Advocate or the Attorney General may refer to it a question whether a bill or any provision of a bill would be within the legislative competence of the Scottish Parliament (section 33(1) of the Scotland Act 1998). Even more significantly, the three devolution statutes relating to Scotland, Northern Ireland and Wales all provide (section 103 of the Scotland Act, section 82 of the Northern Ireland Act and paragraph 32 of schedule 8 to the Government of Wales Act) that any decision of the Privy Council in proceedings under the relevant Acts shall be binding in all legal proceedings (other than proceedings before the Privy Council) involving devolution issues, which may concern the compatibility of a governmental act with the European Convention, and so involve a ruling on human rights,

128

as several devolution issues have already done. While the volume of business generated so far has been relatively modest, this may or may not continue to be so. It is not inconceivable that the number of challenges will increase as the devolved institutions progress from infancy to boundary-testing adolescence. In any event, this new role has inevitably and rightly prompted the question whether it would not make sense in effect to amalgamate the Appellate Committee of the House of Lords and the Judicial Committee of the Privy Council into a single supreme court of the United Kingdom.

Before reviewing the merits of that and other possible models for change, I would like to touch on four matters. First, I recall a cartoon dating from the early 1830s which showed King William IV looking at a placard which bore the words "Reform Bill" and asking "Does that mean me?" It is not immediately flattering to be told that reform is needed either of oneself or of an institution which one serves. So talk of "reforming" the Appellate or Judicial Committee naturally arouses some apprehension among those who sit on them. A call for reform is normally, after all, a response to perceived failure; the police must be reformed because the detection rate is said to be too low and the incidence of sick leave too high; the civil service must be reformed to improve the delivery of government policy; the NHS must be reformed to give quicker, better, more cost-effective treatment; and so on. While of course recognising the undoubted imperfections of our highest courts and laying no claim (personally or collectively) to any infallibility beyond that conferred by finality, I do not myself understand those who call for reform of these courts—or for change, which may be a more neutral term—to be inspired to any great extent by a sense that they are falling down on their duty or failing to fulfil the function they exist to serve.

That leads on to my second point: what function does the Appellate Committee exist to serve in the United Kingdom? This question could be answered at some length, but I will answer it very summarily. The function of the Appellate Committee is, first, to act as the ultimate legal guardian of the constitution; subject to the role of the Judicial Committee in devolution matters; secondly, it is to act (subject to certain qualifications and exceptions) as the ultimate authority on the interpretation and application of the law in these islands. Given the other matters I wish to touch on, I must resist the temptation to elaborate.

Thirdly, I welcome the research which has been done, and is being done, into the structures and working practices of supreme and constitutional courts in other countries. It would be presumptuous and stupid to assume that we have nothing to learn from the experience of others. But it would equally be naïve to suppose that an institution which has developed organically in one country—drawing strength from the tradition, culture and history of that country— can be transplanted to another without a high risk of rejection. Whether one looks at common law countries superficially closest to the United Kingdom—Australia, Canada, New Zealand and the United States—or to our closest European neighbours—France, Germany, Spain—immediate differences spring to mind. We should be willing to learn, but should place no order for carbon paper.

Fourthly, I should acknowledge that many distinguished and knowledgeable people consider that no persuasive case has been made out for any structural change. They include a number of my colleagues, and a number of our predecessors. They include the present government, which has been publicly dismissive of the arguments for change. They include commentators with experience of other systems abroad. There are those who feel, quite strongly, that it is a positive advantage for judges at the highest level to have some exposure to the process of legislation and the conduct of government, an experience in much shorter supply with the decline of political appointments to the bench.

While I respect these opinions—most of them, anyway—I do not agree with them. As I hope is plain, my disagreement is not based on the premise that our highest courts have failed to deliver. It is based on the view that the world has changed and institutions should change with it. To modern eyes, it was always anomalous that a legislative body should exercise judicial power, save in very restricted circumstances. This anomaly may not have mattered in the past. But if the House of Lords is to be reformed, and even if it is not, the opportunity should be taken to reflect in institutional terms what is undoubtedly true in functional terms, that the law lords are judges not legislators and do not belong in a House to whose business they can make no more than a slight contribution.

Among those who favour change, a number of different models have been suggested, each of them capable of variations and each capable of incorporating features of others. I will identify what I see as the four main models, and then comment on each. First is the model already mentioned, an amalgamated Appellate Committee and Judicial Committee acting as the supreme court of the United Kingdom. Second is a new constitutional court of the United Kingdom, operating alongside the existing courts in the three UK jurisdictions. Third is a supreme court on what might be seen as the Luxembourg model, giving authoritative rulings on issues of law referred to it by courts in the three jurisdictions. Fourth is a model differing from existing arrangements inasmuch as the Appellate Committee would be severed from the legislature and established as a court in its own right, re-named and re- housed, but with its powers unchanged and with the Judicial Committee continuing alongside (perhaps with an effectively unified administration) so long as the demand for its separate services continues.

The first (amalgamation) model is certainly the simplest and neatest model. Any bureaucratic reformer would warm to it. But it is probably incapable of achievement. The choice of the Judicial Committee as the forum for resolution of devolution issues was made very deliberately, and there is to my knowledge nothing to suggest that the reasoning which motivated that choice has weakened in any way. It would moreover seem unlikely that the independent states which now appeal to the Privy Council—some of which would wish to continue to do so even if a Caribbean court of final appeal were established—would be content to appeal to a domestic British court, however elevated. So it would seem clear that the Judicial Committee will continue to be needed for the foreseeable future at least. As a final UK court of appeal the Appellate Committee now lacks jurisdiction to hear criminal appeals from Scotland, but it would seem most unlikely that this arrangement will be altered: such jurisdiction has never existed at any time in the past; I am aware of no pressure for change in Scotland; and there is more difference between the criminal laws of Scotland and England than there is between their civil laws, making the House of Lords, with an inevitable majority of non-Scottish members, an inherently unsuitable tribunal for deciding Scottish criminal appeals. So it would seem clear that, whatever form a restructured supreme court may take, there will for the time being continue to be two tribunals, one of them exercising a slightly lop-sided jurisdiction.

In many countries one may find successful and respected constitutional courts, and examples readily spring to mind of courts which perform the functions of a constitutional court although otherwise named. It is therefore right that this option should be considered. Advocates of this model would see virtue in a specialised court which would recruit expert judges and develop a knowledge of the subject more profound than the generality of senior judges could aspire to. I do not myself warm to this suggestion. It would seem to me hard, in the absence of a written constitution, to distinguish clearly between an issue which is constitutional and one which is not, and we could revive the public / private formalism which has disfigured the administration of judicial review. If, as in this country, a constitution is not entrenched, the case for entrusting its final interpretation exclusively to a single tribunal is in my view much weakened. If the existing cadre of supreme court judges is felt to lack constitutional knowledge and expertise—which would perhaps be surprising given their experience in the Privy Council—it can be strengthened. It is, however, salutary, in my opinion, for specialists to be called on to justify their views to sceptical colleagues who may lack their expertise but can bring a more general intelligence to bear on the point at issue and who may be less in thrall than the experts to received opinion and current orthodoxy. To establish a constitutional court would inevitably, I think, be to downgrade the supreme court or courts entrusted with the power of ultimate decision on all non- constitutional questions, and that would in my opinion be a loss. In our own constitutional context I see no advantages in this proposal which would begin to compensate for the disadvantages.

I do not warm either to the proposal that our supreme court be reconstituted on the Luxembourg model, to give binding opinions on issues referred to it by lower courts. That model, as it seems to me, works very well in the European Union: uniformity of interpretation is ensured between one member state and another—an essential condition of an effective union—and the independence and sensitivities of national courts are respected. But the model has little to offer in a domestic context. Appellate courts are usually and rightly restive if asked to decide questions of law without reference to detailed findings of fact, so the need to establish the facts before formulating issues of law would remain. But if the facts have been established, a reference would be little different from an appeal. If the desire is to eliminate intermediate tiers of appeal, that could be achieved by a more elaborate leapfrog procedure, but the very infrequent resort to that procedure does not encourage increased reliance upon it. Again, I see few advantages in this proposal.

So my own personal preference would be for the fourth model: a supreme court severed from the legislature, established as a court in its own right, re-named and appropriately re- housed, properly equipped and resourced and affording facilities for litigants, judges and staff such as, in most countries of the world, are taken for granted. As indicated, I envisage the Judicial Committee continuing alongside (perhaps with an effectively unified administration) so long as the demand for its separate services continues.

To many, mention of a supreme court conjures up visions of the world's best-known supreme court, that of the United States, striking down and annulling congressional legislation and asserting the primacy of the constitution. I wish to make plain that a supreme court of the United Kingdom could neither claim nor exercise such a power. Under our constitutional dispensation Parliament is sovereign. We have no entrenched constitution to which primacy could be accorded. Thus the changes I favour would not lead to enhancement of the existing powers of the House: the gain would lie in regularisation and rationalisation of the constitutional position of the supreme court and (it would be hoped) improved facilities leading to a clear enhancement of its operational efficiency.

I hope you will bear with me if I touch, necessarily quite briefly, on four questions which have, quite properly, been discussed in the literature on this subject.

1. Should appeal to the supreme court be as of right or subject to the grant of leave, and if the latter which courts should be empowered to grant leave? At present, appeals from Scotland require no leave. But there are only a handful of Scottish appeals each year and the absence of a leave filter causes no practical problem. In England and Wales and Northern Ireland leave is required, and may be given either by the court appealed from (although it rarely is) or by an appeal committee of the House. I am very clearly of opinion that since the House can, under existing arrangements, hear only some 60-80 full appeals a year, there must be a power to decide which those cases should be. If,

as in many countries in Europe and elsewhere, there existed an unfettered right of appeal, the inevitable consequence would be the summary dismissal of the overwhelming majority of those appeals, probably on paper without a hearing. I doubt whether such a process would be very satisfying to litigants brought up in our tradition. I would not for my part echo the criticism, sometimes heard, that the Court of Appeal is nowadays too reluctant to grant leave: no division of that court can know what other cases are competing for the attention of the House, and the decision is usually best left to the House unless considerations of time weigh in favour of immediate leave. If the Court of Appeal considers the case to be one which probably does merit consideration by the House, it can helpfully give its reasons for holding that opinion when refusing leave and the House will then have the benefit of its view.

2. What should be the criterion or criteria for granting leave? This is a question which has been much discussed, and rightly so, since the grant (or refusal) of leave may have very significant consequences for the parties and for the wider public. The Standing Orders of the House at present provide that

> "Leave is granted to petitions which raise an arguable point of law of general public importance which ought to be considered by the House at that time, bearing in mind that the cause will have already been the subject of judicial decision."

This form of words highlights three features of the current test, all of them important. First, the function of the House is to resolve vexed questions of law. Where the law is clear the House has ordinarily no role to play. It is not its function to correct misapplications of settled law. That is one function (among others) of the Court of Appeal, which should be relied on to discharge it. Second, the point of law should ordinarily be one of importance to the wider public and not simply to the immediate parties. Third, the case should provide a suitable vehicle for deciding the point of law in question. A case may be thought not to do so, whether because of findings of fact made in the case, or because it may be decided on other grounds, or because it appears oppressive to subject the particular parties to further expense, or for a number of other possible reasons.

I am of course aware of criticisms: that the test is not applied with complete consistency; that on occasion leave is refused to challenge a decision which is shortly thereafter overruled in another case (an experience which I have myself shared with other practitioners, and which certainly leaves a residue of dissatisfaction); that of two cases raising the same or a similar point leave is given in one and refused in another; that leave is refused in cases where it should be given and given in cases where it should not. These are undoubted blemishes, which every effort should be and is made to address. One suggested solution is to circulate all petition papers to all members of the court. This is the practice, as I understand, with the 5000 petitions presented annually to the US Supreme Court. But one has to wonder how much attention the individual judges are able to give to so large a number of petitions. It seems at least possible that in many cases the law clerks must exercise an effective power of decision. The House is not, happily, burdened with anything approaching that number of petitions, but I wonder if the detailed consideration given by three judges forming an appeal committee to the petitions for leave allocated to them is not a more effective procedure than  a less detailed consideration by all the members of the court. If all the members were to give the same detailed scrutiny to all the petitions as the appeal committee now give, it would make large inroads on the time available for hearing and resolving substantive appeals. These are, I think, difficult and important questions, meriting further consideration and comparative research.

It is often urged that appeal committees should give reasons when refusing leave. The long- standing practice has been not to do so in the generality of cases, and there appear to be no Convention reasons for altering it. I would not favour alteration. Where leave is refused on paper at the outset, it indicates the appeal committee's clear view that the published test is not met. If the respondent's objections are invited and leave is then refused, it is because the appeal committee is persuaded (or any doubt dispelled) by the objections. Where there is an oral hearing and leave is refused, I doubt if experienced counsel are often in much doubt about the reason for refusal. If it were the invariable practice to give reasons the risk would, I think, arise that either the reasons given would be so summary and formulaic as to be unhelpful or, if they were more detailed, that the task would occupy a considerable amount of time better used in other ways.

3. Should all the law lords (by which I mean the 12 Lords of Appeal in Ordinary) sit together to hear every case? This is of course the practice in many, perhaps most, supreme courts, as in the United States. It contrasts with our own practice of hearing appeals before committees of 5, and on relatively rare occasions 7. Those who favour the whole court approach rely

on an essentially very simple argument. They point out that judges are individual human beings, not automata or slot-machines. However true they may be to their judicial oaths, they inevitably bring their own individual philosophies, thought processes and casts of mind to the judicial bench. Thus if a case is heard by a sub-group of judges, the outcome may depend on the membership of the sub-group. The only way of ensuring that the ultimate decision represents the opinion of the court is to ensure that all members of the court are party to it.

The rate of dissent in the House of Lords is in fact very low, much lower than in the US Supreme Court or the High Court of Australia. The great majority of decisions are unanimous. So they are in the Privy Council, where the right to dissent is now recognised but not very often exercised. But cases do arise, however few in number, in which the presence of X or the absence of Y could affect the outcome of a case decided on a bare majority. This possibility could indeed be excluded if all the judges, including X and Y, heard every case.

It would in some ways be attractive to adopt this practice. But it would be subject to any one or more of a number of drawbacks. The cadre of 12 appointed Lords of Appeal in Ordinary (a cohort usually reduced to 11 and often to 10 through absences in Londonderry or Hong Kong or elsewhere) currently provides the nucleus of one or two appellate committees in the House and one in the Privy Council. If all the law lords were to hear every case, the most immediate and obvious result would be a savage reduction in the number of cases heard, probably by well over half. It would be possible to mitigate this result to some extent by resorting to one or other or both of two expedients much relied on elsewhere: drastic reduction of oral hearing times; and heavy reliance on legal assistants, not only as researchers, collators and note makers but also as the authors of judgments. Now I would accept that in a number of cases the time allowed for oral argument, already reduced as compared with 30 or 40 years ago, could be reduced further without severe loss, and the introduction of legal assistants (both in the Court of Appeal and the House of Lords) has proved so obviously successful that in future we are likely to seek the help of more of them. It would, however, be a source of profound regret to me, and I feel sure a large majority of my colleagues, if we were constrained to restrict oral argument to 30 minutes or so a side and if we reached the point where the written judgment in the case was wholly or substantially the work of a law clerk or legal assistant. However well these practices work in other legal systems—and I cast no aspersion on them—I would wish to cling to the tradition of full, but lean, oral argument (building on written arguments already supplied) and to the tradition that the eventual judgment, however poor a thing, is the judge's own.

There is in my opinion a further potential drawback to the whole court approach. If all the members of a court decide all the cases, the opportunity arises for the appointing authority to seek quite deliberately to influence the course of the court's decision-making in one direction or another when filling vacancies in the court. Examples readily spring to mind of jurisdictions in which this is avowedly done. Here, for the last half century at least, the practice has been to make appointments on the basis of an appointee's perceived merit, record and experience, without regard to his or her position on any political, social or other spectrum. The question how a potential appointee might be likely to decide any major legal issue of the day is not considered. For us, in our situation, this seems to me a source of strength.

I would accept, as has been suggested, that the House should perhaps be more ready than it is to sit in enlarged committees where the case for whatever reason warrants it. But I think on balance that any advantage of an invariable practice of hearing all cases before all the law lords (even if the overall number were reduced, as it would have to be) would be heavily outweighed by the disadvantages. That conclusion leads on to my fourth and last question.

4. How are the law lords selected to sit on particular appeals? I think it important that the procedure be clearly understood. Forthcoming appeals are allotted dates, taking account of counsel's time estimates, by the Judicial Office of the House of Lords and the Registrar of the Judicial Committee. Officials then prepare a draft programme assigning law lords to cases. This draft programme is given to the two most senior law lords with enough material to enable them to understand the nature of the cases listed. A meeting is then held attended by these two law lords, the head of the Judicial Office and the Registrar (but no one else) to review the draft programme. The object of this meeting is to match horses to courses, that is, to try and ensure that so far as possible every committee includes members with specialised expertise and experience in the field to which the appeal relates, in addition of course to members with more general experience. There are a number of other matters which affect the outcome: the desirability of including Scottish and Northern Irish law lords in committees hearing appeals from those jurisdictions respectively; unavailability; any conflict to which any law lord may

be subject; the desirability of achieving some balance, for individual law lords, between sittings in the House and in the Privy Council; the work loads of individual law lords; and so on. The likely outcome of any appeal, or the possible effect of it, is not considered. Neither in its draft nor in its revised form is the programme the subject of consultation with or approval by anyone I have not mentioned. Inevitably, the programme, even in its final form, may have to be changed, sometimes at short notice, for a variety of reasons of which illness is the most obvious. The constitution of forthcoming committees is not a secret: any litigant or practitioner wishing to know the constitution of a committee due to hear a particular appeal can, on telephoning the relevant office, receive the best information then available.

I am very conscious that I have failed to touch on a number of interesting and important questions discussed in the literature and other addresses on this topic. But I have tried to indicate why, in my opinion, change is desirable and to describe the course which change should take. Our object is plain enough: to ensure that our supreme court is so structured and equipped as best to fulfil its functions and to command the confidence of the country in the changed world in which we live. The Constitution Unit has performed an invaluable service by stimulating debate on the form which change should take. But inertia, I suggest, is not an option.

# Index

144

146